Love

Thread through the Bible

JEANETTA WATKINS

Order from:

Jeanetta Watkins
4873 Heifner Road
Adamsville, Alabama 35005

© 2004 Jeanetta Watkins

Publisher's Cataloging-in-Publication Data

Watkins, Jeanetta
Thread through the Bible: God's handiwork./
Jeanetta Watkins.
112 pp; 21.59 cm.
Thirteen chapters—Questions.
1. Love. 2. Women—Christian Life
I. Watkins, Jeanetta. II. Title.
ISBN 0-9755962-0-9
248.8

Printed in the United States

CONTENTS

Lesson 1

WHAT IS THIS THING CALLED LOVE?

In this series we will examine what I've called the *Thread through the Bible*. From the first chapter of Genesis through the last chapter of Revelation, the scriptures are filled with encouragement and admonitions for us to love our fellow human beings. Love is the continuing factor throughout the scriptures. We will examine three avenues by which women can show love in this world:

> Hospitality
> Evangelism
> Benevolence

While the woman's role is different from the man's, God still expects her to do her best and use all the talents He has left in her keeping. The parable of the talents (Matthew 25) is not a lesson just for men. Romans 14:12 reads, "So then each of us shall give account of himself to God." And again in 2 Corinthians 5:10:

> For we must all be made manifest before the judgment-seat of Christ; that each one may receive the things done in the body, according to what he has done, whether it be good or bad.

We, as women, cannot get to heaven on some else's good deeds. While we understand that eternal life is given by the grace of God (Ephesians 2:8), and that we at our best are unprofitable servants (Luke 17:10), the Lord does require each of His children to believe on Him (John 6:29), be filled with good works (1 Timothy 2:10), bear fruit (John 15:8), and grow spiritually (1 Peter 2:2). All of these things combined will save us in glory. The dear apostle John says, "Blessed are they that do his commandments that they may have right to the tree of life, and may enter in through the gates into the city" (Revelation 22:14).

Jesus died so that we could live eternally. We are told that salvation is a "free gift of God" (Romans 6:23). Does this mean we can just sit back and do nothing? Definitely not! Hebrews 11:6 says that "without faith it is impossible to please Him."

Since faith is belief of things not seen, does this mean we just have to believe Christ is who He claimed to be, and salvation is assured? James 2:26 says no: "For just as the body without the spirit is dead; so also, faith without works is dead." How then can we reconcile the fact that salvation is a free gift, but we must work for salvation? Jesus answers that question.

> He who has My commandments and keeps them is the one who loves Me; and he who loves Me will be loved by My Father, and I will love him and will disclose Myself to him (John 14:21).

John tells us,

> If we say that we have fellowship with Him and yet walk in the darkness, we lie and do not practice the truth; but if we walk in the Light as He Himself is in the Light, we have fellowship with one another, and the blood of Jesus His Son cleanses us from all sin (1 John 1:6–7).

As we begin to try to understand the depths of love, let's do the exercise below. Before you read any further, get a pen and write your first name in all of the blanks.

_____ suffers long and is kind. _____ does not envy. _____ does not parade herself, _____ is not puffed up; _____ does not behave rudely, _____ does not seek her own, _____ is not provoked and thinks no evil. _____ does not rejoice in iniquity, but rejoices in the truth; _____ bears all things, _____ believes all things, _____ hopes all things, _____ endures all things. When _____ was a child she spoke as a child, she understood as a child, she thought as a child; but when _____ became a woman she put away childish things.

The above paragraph is a paraphrase of sentences found 1 Corinthians 13:4–11. We usually turn to this passage when we want to understand the meaning of the word *love* more completely.

If you study from the old King James translation you will notice the word used in place of love is charity. In the year 1611 (when the translation was created) *charity* was translated from the Latin word *carita*, which means "dearness, affection, high regard." Today *charity* is used to show acts of benevolence toward others. The word Paul used, in the original Greek text is *agape*, which means "unselfish, loyal, and benevolent concern for the well-being of another" *(Holman Bible Dictionary)*. So we can readily see that the correct translation of the word in this passage is "love."

Just as we all look different from each other, we also have different strengths and weaknesses. Maybe one person has no trouble being kind but is short on patience. Someone else, on the other hand, may be very patient but has a problem with jealousy.

In the next few lessons we will examine the ideal traits of love more closely. We will also study how we can incorporate them into our lives in order to reach the level of love Christ wants us to attain.

Some people think that until the time of Christianity Jews were taught to love only their fellow Hebrews—they were to treat Gentiles and Samaritans as they would treat dogs (Matthew 15:26). Several passages in the Old Testament refute this theory.

- Leviticus 19:18—"You shall not take vengeance, nor bear any grudge against the children of your people, but you shall love your neighbor as yourself."

- Leviticus 19:34—"The stranger [Gentile] who dwells among you shall be to you as one born among you, and you shall love him as yourself; for you were strangers in the land of Egypt: I am the Lord your God."

- Deuteronomy 10:19—"Therefore love the stranger, for you were strangers in the land of Egypt."

- Proverbs 24:17—"Do not rejoice when your enemy falls, and do not let your heart be glad when he stumbles."

- Finally we read: "He who does not love does not know God, for God is love (1 John 4:8).

In 1 Corinthians 13 the word *love* is given personification, and becomes a noun. We learn how godly love is supposed to behave. In other passages we also notice that *love* is a verb, not a feeling or an emotion. Dig back to your elementary school grammar classes. Webster defines a verb as "a word that expresses action." When Peter told the Lord he loved him, Jesus followed up by giving him something to do: "Feed My Lambs . . . Tend My sheep . . . Feed My sheep" (John 21:15–17).

A number of years ago I spoke with a shepherd who lived in Bonifay, Florida. He said this passage has a deeper meaning for him than it would for those not familiar with sheep.

The word translated "feed" in verse 15 is from the Greek word *bosko*. This means "to pasture, to fodder, to feed, to keep." This indicates feeding with a little extra care. That makes sense when you think about it. Lambs would require more care than full-grown sheep.

The word translated "tend" in verse 16 is from the Greek word *poimaino* and means "to tend as a shepherd, feed (cattle), rule." This carries the idea of pasturing a flock, finding a grassy, safe area where the sheep can graze. Once there, they would require relatively little supervision. (If you are using the old King James translation, *poimaino* is translated "feed" in this verse.)

The word for "feed" in verse 17 is exactly the same word used in verse 15, when speaking of feeding the lambs. We can conclude that some sheep require more care than others. The shepherd explained that this is true with older sheep. Their teeth are worn down from years of grazing, so they have a problem getting enough to eat in a pasture. Consequently, a shepherd will supplement their diet with softer fodder. The Florida shepherd went on to reveal that older ewes are worth the extra effort because they almost always produce twins. That extra lamb means extra money in the shepherd's pocket. He drew the following conclusions from his knowledge of sheep.

- The lambs can be compared to the babes in Christ. They need to be taught slowly, allowing time for growth. Peter said, "As newborn babes, desire the pure milk of the word, that you may grow thereby" (1 Peter 2:2).

- The mature sheep are compared to the full grown Christian. They need to be working and exercising their spiritual senses, so they might grow into productive workers in the kingdom of the Lord. We read in Hebrews 5:14: "But solid food belongs to those who are of full age, that is, those who by reason of use have their senses exercised to discern both good and evil."

- The old sheep compare to the aged Christians in the church. They cannot carry the workload they once did. They might need someone to give them a ride to worship, or take them to visit other members. This extra care will pay off for the one who renders the service because of the rich fountain of wisdom and experience possessed by those who have spent a lifetime as Christians.

If we really love our neighbors, we will be able to work out petty differences that might come up from time to time. If we really love our husbands, we will be able to solve any misunderstandings that get in the way of our relationship with them. If we really love our children, we will be patient and understanding parents—bringing them up "in the training and admonition of the Lord." If we really love lost souls, we will have no problem telling others about the "hope that lies within us" (1 Peter 3:15).

John summed it up in 1 John 4:7–8:

Beloved, let us love one another, for love is of God; and everyone who loves is born of God and knows God. He who does not love does not know God, for God is love.

Study Questions

1. In this book, what three avenues are we going to study, through which women show love? _____
_____

2. Why is it so important that we learn what God has to say about love? _____
_____

3. What passage do you turn to when you want to examine the attributes of true love? _____

4. In 1 Corinthians 13 the King James translation of 1611 uses the word *charity*. From what language was that word translated into English? _____

5. In the shepherd's explanation of John 21:15–17, what do the three types of sheep represent? _____
_____
_____

6. What is not known by the person who does not love?
_____ Why? _____
_____

7. What are the two greatest commandments? (Mark 12:30–31).

   (1) _____

   (2) _____

8. What level of perfection did Jesus wait for the people on earth to attain before He left heaven and died on the cross for their salvation? (Romans 5:8).
_____

9. What is the meaning of unconditional love?

_____

Lesson 2

The Circle of Love

We all know that we are supposed to love God; that goes without question. Did you realize, however, that in order to love God we must love each other? We read in 1 John 4:20: "If someone says, 'I love God.' and hates his brother, he is a liar; for he who does not love his brother whom he has seen, how can he love God whom he has not seen?" In addition, we must love ourselves if we are to know how to love each other. In Mark 12:31 Jesus says, "And you shall love your neighbor as yourself." It follows then that since we are to love others as we love ourselves, we must learn to love ourselves first. In fact, biblical love forms a circle, and a break in that circle causes a lack of the kind of love God wants His children to demonstrate.

When I say we are to love ourselves, I'm not talking about a stuck-up or haughty attitude. Romans 12:3 warns:

> For I say, through the grace given to me, to everyone who is among you, not to think of himself more highly than he ought to think, but to think soberly, as God has dealt to each one a measure of faith.

What I am talking about is taking pride in who we are and what, with God's help, we can become.

Another term that describes this attitude is *self-esteem,* and if anyone has reason to be proud of who she is and her worth, it is a Christian. Mature Christians know that this godly pride is sorely lacking among many women in the church of the Lord.

Before we can love anyone to the fullest extent, we must become genuinely acquainted with that person. But first, we must really get to know ourselves if we are to have the kind of self-assurance God wants us to have. In Philippians 2:12 Paul tells us: "Therefore, my beloved ... work out your own salvation with fear and trembling." We also read: "Examine yourselves as to whether you are in the faith. Test yourselves" (2 Corinthians 13:5). From these scriptures, we can see that we are to scrutinize ourselves, examine ourselves, and ask ourselves questions. (No, it's not a sign of senility to talk to yourself once in a while).

Next, if we are to be the kind of person God would have us to be, we must be satisfied with who we are—in spite of our faults. How many times have you heard someone begin a statement with: "If I were a man ... If I were president ... If I were rich ..."—or any other host of things—"I would do something great." We need to learn the same thing Paul learned and so stated in Philippians 4:11: "Not that I speak in regard to need, for I have learned in whatever state I am, to be content." Notice that Paul was not born with contentment; he had to learn it. Perhaps we haven't reached the point of maturity that Paul had reached, but we can learn if we really want to.

It is in our best interest—not to speak of being pleasing to God—to grow toward perfection. In 1 Timothy 6:6 we read: "Now godliness with contentment is great gain." Being contented does not mean we are always pleased with the way everything is going. It is, rather, not becoming overly anxious about any situation in which we have done all we know to do and it still won't go away. We must learn to "run the race" (Hebrews 12:1) and leave the rest to God, since Jesus is "the author and finisher of our faith" (Hebrews 12:2). As we begin to learn how to love each other, keep in mind that the same attitudes we are supposed to have toward each other apply to ourselves as well.

Study Questions

1. According to 1 John 4:20, what must we do before we can truly love God? _____

2. According to Mark 12:31, how much are we to love our neighbor? _____

3. What is another term used to signify taking pride in one's self? _____

4. What passage would you use to show that we are not to be stuck-up or haughty? _____

5. Who are we supposed to examine (test) to see if that person is "in the faith"? _____

6. What words did God use to describe the woman He created? (cf. Genesis 1:31.) _____

_____

7. How are we able (even as mortal women) to do "all things"? (cf. Philippians 4:13.) _____

_____

8. According to Philippians 4:11, what trait can we learn that will help us cope with the many difficulties of life?

_____

9. What three individuals form the "Circle of Love"?

_____

10. What do the scriptures say about someone who claims to love God but hates his brother? _____

_____

11. Does one acquire godly love for each other naturally?

_____

Explain: _____

_____

_____

_____

Lesson 3

HOSPITALITY—AN OUTWARD SIGN OF LOVE

We saw in the first lesson that love is a verb, and that its actions do not result merely from emotions. If we say we love each other and do nothing, we fall short of the Lord's expectations. The first activity of love we will study is hospitality. What does hospitality have to do with love?

Let's allow the Bible to answer that question for us. In the New Testament, Jesus explains how He looks at it when we do something good for someone else: "And the King will answer and say to them, 'Assuredly, I say to you, inasmuch as you did it to one of the least of these My brethren, you did it to Me'" (Matthew 25:40). We need to internalize the thought that whatever we do to others, we do it to our Savior. We are taught: "With goodwill doing service, as to the Lord" (Ephesians 6:7) and "Whatever you do, do it heartily, as to the Lord and not to men" (Colossians 3:23). How would you like to have Jesus over for a cup of coffee or a meal? Wouldn't that be great? Well, He's said that whatever we do for others we do for Him.

Who should be the recipient of our good deeds? Our family . . . our close friends . . . those with whom we have something in common? The answer is all of the above and even more. Even in the Old Testament (Leviticus 19:33–34 and Deuteronomy 10:18–19) God told the Israelites, specifically, how to treat strangers with whom they might come in contact. It's easy to do good to, and love those who are most like us, but the Lord expects—yea, demands—even more. In 1 Peter 4:9 we are not only commanded to be hospitable, but we are also told what our attitude must be while we perform this act of love. Let's examine some examples of some people in the scriptures who practiced hospitality.

Entertaining Angels (Hebrews 13:2)

How would you feel about feeding an angel? Would you offer an excuse why he couldn't sit at your table and share your meal? While the age of miracles has passed, the providence of God will continue until the end of time. Let's look at some examples of people who have entertained angels unaware.

Abraham

Abraham showed hospitality to the three men who came by his home one day:

> Please let a little water be brought, and wash your feet, and rest yourselves under the tree. And I will bring a morsel of bread, that you may refresh your hearts. After that you may pass by, inasmuch as you have come to your servant (Genesis 18:1–8).

It seemed that he was asking them if they would allow him to do this thing as a favor to himself, instead of a service to the travelers. Abraham knew what we all must learn, if we are to be pleasing to the Lord. When we do something good for others, we are the ones who are blessed. In Acts 20:35 Paul quotes Jesus as saying, "It is more blessed to give than to receive." When he saw the visitors he had no idea they were angels, or that they had come to bring him the wonderful news that he and Sarah would have a son.

Lot

In Genesis 19:1–8 we read about Lot and his attitude toward two visitors who dropped by his home in the wicked city of Sodom. Unknown to him, these were also angels, but Lot insisted that they spend the night at his house. Many generations after this event, Peter reminds us of him and his problems by saying, "For that righteous man, dwelling among them, tormented his righteous soul from day to day by seeing and hearing their lawless deeds" (2 Peter 2:8).

Manoah

In Judges 13:15–16 when an Angel came to Manoah and his wife to tell them of the impending birth of Samson, they offered him hospitality, but he refused their offer. Manoah said to the Angel of the Lord,

> "Please let us detain you, and we will prepare a young goat for you." And the Angel of the Lord said to Manoah, "Though you detain Me, I will not eat your food. But if you offer a burnt offering, you must offer it to the Lord." (For Manoah did not know He was the Angel of the Lord.)

Sacrifice in Offering Hospitality

The Widow of Zarephath

In 1 Kings 17 we read of a widow who lived in Zarephath. Because of the famine, she had used up all her food stores, and Elijah came by and asked for something to eat. She explained there was only enough food for one meal, and then she and her son were prepared to die. However, when he told her to make him a small cake first, she complied. It's easy enough to be generous when there will be plenty left over for us, but godly love sometimes requires sacrifice.

As it turned out, she was blessed far more than she could have ever imagined. This prophet of God worked a miracle that kept her fed throughout this time of need.

The Shunammite Couple

Elisha was traveling throughout the countryside and encountered a woman in Shunem. She and her husband went out of their way to make this man of God feel welcome. We find the story in 2 Kings 4:8–10:

> Now it happened one day that Elisha went to Shunem, where there was a notable woman, and she persuaded him to eat some food. So it was, as often as he passed by, he would turn in there to eat some food. And she said to her husband, "Look now, I know that this is a holy man of God, who passes by us regularly. Please, let us make a small upper room on the wall; and let us put a bed for him there, and a table and a chair and a lampstand; so it will be, whenever he comes to us, he can turn in there."

One thing you might notice is that it was the woman who instigated this relationship. As a general rule, most men are too busy with other things to be bothered with these details, so such decisions are up to the woman of the house. Certainly, she should not go against her husband's wishes regarding who is invited into the home, but she should (if God's will is to be done) do what she can.

True, the Shunammite family practiced the ultimate display of hospitality, and not many of us could build an addition on the house to make room for travelers. However, my husband and I knew a family, several years ago near Cincinnati, Ohio, who actually did that. They turned some unused attic space into a small bedroom and sitting room just so they could ask visiting preachers to spend the night with them. We were fortunate enough to be asked to stay with these good Christians, and we were treated with all the kindliness you'd expect from your own family. We will never forget their thoughtfulness.

Jason

In the New Testament we find a man named Jason. He showed hospitality to the apostle Paul and his companions. As a result of his harboring Paul, the Jews handled him roughly and brought charges against him to the rulers of the city. Read about this incident in Acts 17.

Jesus and His Attitude about Hospitality

Jesus as a Guest

From the beginning of the ministry of Jesus, hospitality played an important role in those who followed His teachings. In Luke 9:2–3 Jesus sent His disciples to spread the gospel. When He sent them out He said, "Take nothing for the journey, neither staffs nor bag nor bread nor money; and do not have two tunics apiece." We can conclude from the information given that they were to rely on the hospitality of those with whom they studied and taught the gospel.

Jesus did much of His teaching while eating and drinking with those who needed spiritual guidance. In Mark 2:16 the scribes and Pharisees condemned Him for eating with the tax collectors and sinners. Jesus answered their criticism by saying, "Those who are well have no need of a physician, but those who are sick. I did not come to call the righteous, but sinners, to repentance" (Mark 2:18).

If the occasion called for it, Jesus took the initiative and invited himself to someone's home. When Zacchaeus climbed the tree, to get a better look at the Savior, the Lord said, "Zacchaeus, make haste and come down, for today I must stay at your house" (Luke 19:5).

We find that Jesus felt particularly close to a family in Bethany, namely Lazarus, Mary, and Martha. We can come to this conclusion as we read in John 11:3: "Therefore the sisters sent to Him, saying, 'Lord, behold, he whom You love is sick.'" Again, in John 12:1, we find the Lord visiting the same area:

> Then, six days before the Passover, Jesus came to Bethany, where Lazarus was who had been dead, whom He had raised from the dead. There they made Him a supper; and Martha served.

Jesus as a Host

On several occasions, Jesus played host, even if He had nowhere to lay his head. In Matthew 14:19 we read,

> Then He commanded the multitudes to sit down on the grass. And He took the five loaves and the two fish, and looking up to heaven, He blessed and broke and gave the loaves to the disciples; and the disciples gave to the multitudes.

In Matthew 15:36 we also note: "And He took the seven loaves and the fish and gave thanks, broke them and gave them to His disciples; and the disciples gave to the multitude."

In John 21:9–13 Jesus not only fed His disciples, but He apparently cooked the food Himself.

> Then, as soon as they had come to land, they saw a fire of coals there, and fish laid on it, and bread . . . Jesus said to them, "Bring some of the fish which you have just caught." . . . Jesus then came and took the bread and gave it to them, and likewise the fish.

(Could we wrest the scriptures here and say this gives us biblical authority for men to do the cooking? Just kidding!)

Jesus did much of His teaching while eating and drinking with those who needed spiritual guidance (Matthew 11:19; Mark 2:16). When Zacchaeus climbed the tree to get a better look at the Savior, Jesus said, "Zacchaeus, make haste and come down, for today I must stay at your house" (Luke 19:5). We find Him, on another occasion, being condemned for eating with tax collectors and sinners (Matthew 11:19).

Early Christians Practiced Hospitality

When the church was established in Jerusalem, these new Christians were anxious to be together and enjoy the blessings they had found in Jesus. "So continuing daily with one accord in the temple, and breaking bread from house to house, they ate their food with gladness and simplicity of heart" (Acts 2:46).

Aquila and Priscilla

We first met this couple in Acts 18 when they were living in Corinth after they, and all other Roman Jews, had been evicted from their homes in Rome. Most of us would have spent our time feeling bitter about our situation if we had been forced to leave our country and relocate in a foreign land. However, these two Christians didn't have time for pity parties; they were too busy doing the Lord's work. They opened their home to the apostle Paul, showing him hospitality and assistance in his ministry. In fact, they traveled some with him and helped with the teaching. We find in Acts 18:26 that they took aside an eloquent preacher, Apollos, and instructed him in "the way of the Lord more perfectly."

Lydia

In Acts 16 we meet a businesswoman named Lydia. When Paul and his companions first encountered her, she was at the riverbank with other women having, what we might call, a prayer meeting. After she learned the truth and became a Christian, she told the men, "If you have judged me to be faithful to the Lord, come to my house and stay." This was not just an off-handed invitation because Paul goes on to say, "And she persuaded us."

A Philippian Warden

When Paul and Silas were freed from prison in Philippi, the jailer took them to his home, washed their stripes, and made them comfortable. After obeying the gospel, he invited them into his house and set food before them (Acts 16).

Phoebe

In Romans 16:1–2 we meet a woman named Phoebe. Paul tells the church in Rome: "I commend to you Phoebe our sister, who is a servant of the church in Cenchrea . . . for indeed she has been a helper of many and of myself also."

Publius

When Paul and his companions were teaching on the island of Malta, they became acquainted with an influential man who showed them true hospitality. We read in Acts 28:7: "In that region there was an estate of the leading citizen of the island, whose name was Publius, who received us and entertained us courteously for three days."

Onesiphorus

In 2 Timothy 1:16 Paul praises a man who had shown him hospitality in the past: "The Lord grant mercy to the household of Onesiphorus, for he often refreshed me, and was not ashamed of my chain."

Study Questions

1. When we show love to each other by demonstrating the active love taught in the scriptures, or fail to show love, how does Jesus look at our actions?

   _____

2. What three things did God command the Israelites to do for strangers (non-Jews)?

   _____

   _____

   _____

3. Whatever we find to do, how are we supposed to do it?

   _____

   As though we were doing it to whom? _____

4. Who dropped in to visit Abraham and Sarah?_____

   _____

5. What news did these strangers bring to Abraham and his wife? _____

   _____

6. Did Lot's visitors bring him good news, like they had to his Uncle Abraham? _____

7. What was their message to Lot? _____

   _____

8. Did the stranger accept Manoah's offer of hospitality?

   _____

9. Because of her sacrifice, what did Elijah, by the power of God, do for the widow of Zarephath?

_____

_____

10. What did a couple who lived in Shunem do to show their hospitality to Elisha?

_____

11. When Jesus sent the twelve out to preach the gospel, how were they to support themselves on this journey?

_____

12. Who invited Jesus to the home of Zacchaeus?

_____

13. List some ways that the Lord showed hospitality to others, even though He had no home?

_____

_____

_____

14. When the church was first established in Jerusalem, how often did these new Christians get together for fellowship?

_____

15. What was Aquila and Priscilla's situation when we meet them in Acts 18?

_____

16. Who was Lydia and what was her attitude toward hospitality?

_____

_____

Lesson 4

HOSPITALITY IS NOT AN OPTION

In Romans 12:10–13 hospitality is coupled with brotherly love. The apostles admonished the Christians in Rome: "Be kindly affectionate to one another with brotherly love . . . given to hospitality." (Note: "Given to" means "to practice, follow, run after.") Again we see in 1 Peter 4:9 that we are not only to be hospitable but we are to do it "without grumbling."

Required of "Widows Indeed"
When Paul was instructing the churches which widows would be qualified to be "numbered"—this simply means that the church provided their physical needs—he said only those would be qualified who had, among many other things, "lodged strangers" (1 Timothy 5:10).

Required of Elders
In 1 Timothy 3:2, the qualifications for elders in the church are listed: "A bishop then must be blameless, the husband of one wife, temperate, sober-minded, of good behavior, hospitable, able to teach."

Paul addresses the same subject as he writes to Titus:

For a bishop must be blameless, as a steward of God, not self-willed, not quick-tempered, not given to wine, not violent, not greedy for money, but hospitable, a lover of what is good, sober-minded, just, holy, self-controlled (Titus 1:7–8).

Opportunities and Responsibilities

God gives us opportunities to exercise our talents, and He expects us to use those abilities. However, He also made us free moral agents, and we can refuse to do our duty and bury our talent in the ground. When the master returned home he called the servant who had hidden his talent and said, "You wicked and lazy servant" (Matthew 25:26). We might say, "He didn't steal the Lord's money; he didn't treat anyone unkindly; he didn't set out to do wrong, so how does that make him wicked?" Wickedness equals sinfulness and sin cannot inherit the kingdom of heaven (1 Corinthians 6:9).

In addition to those who are lazy, God also despises those who just plod along in the middle of the road without actually getting too involved. They want the blessings of a Christian without any of the responsibilities. The church of Laodicea had this particular problem. God hated it so badly He told them, "I will spit you out of my mouth" (Revelation 3:16).

God expects us to get involved. He expects us to give a task a hundred percent of our strength. In Esther 4:14 Mordecai told his cousin Queen Esther,

> For if you remain completely silent at this time, relief and deliverance will arise for the Jews from another place … Yet who knows whether you have come to the kingdom for such a time as this?

How do you know that God didn't put you in your present situation so you would have an opportunity to grow spiritually?

In 1 Timothy 5:14 Paul admonishes the younger women to "manage the house." Certainly, this places responsibility for initiating responsibility on the woman. True, she cannot go against her husband's wishes, and I have known a few men who refused to let their wives invite folks into their home, but this is the rare exception, not the rule.

The story is told about a tombstone that was discovered in a small Kentucky cemetery. Below a woman's name, the date of her birth and the date of her death is a simple six-word epitaph, "She done the best she could." Can anyone hope to do anything beyond that? The Lord doesn't expect more than anyone is capable of producing, but He does expect us to put forth our very best effort.

Whatever happened to families keeping the preacher during a gospel meeting. It has evolved into making a reservation at a local motel, and making arrangements for him to put his meals on the motel bill. Some congregations have a pot luck dinner each evening before time for services, but that's not done in a lot of locations.

Where are hospitable men like Abraham, Lot, and Manoah? Where are the women like Lydia, Mary, and Martha, who are willing to open their homes and hearts? Where are the couples like the Shunammite couple, who made the Lord's prophet feel at home? Where are couples like Paul's fellow workers, Priscilla and Aquila?

Before you say it, I know you are busy. I know times have changed, but God's word remains the same. If you and your husband have to go to work, give the visiting preacher a key and show him where the food is kept. Ladies, you will never feel more blessed than when you bring a visiting preachers, and sometimes their families, into your homes for a few days. I grew up in a family that felt it was an honor to keep the preacher. Friendships were made during those days that will last throughout eternity. This man is your brother. Treat him like family.

Blessings

In Romans 10:14–15 we read a passage that shows how God looks at the vocation of preaching the gospel:

How then shall they call on Him in whom they have not believed? And how shall they believe in Him of whom they have not heard? And how shall they hear without a preacher? And how shall they preach unless they are sent? As it is written: "How beautiful are the feet of those who preach the gospel of peace, who bring glad tidings of good things!"

Speaking to those He sent out to preach, Jesus said, "For whoever gives you a cup of water to drink in My name, because you belong to Christ, assuredly, I say to you, he will by no means lose his reward" (Mark 9:41).

Study Questions

1. How are we to show hospitality? (See 1 Peter 4:9.)

   _____

2. What two things did the Lord call the servant who hid his talent? _____

   _____

3. How might we use Mordecai's logic toward Esther on ourselves? _____

   _____

4. Widows who were to be supported by the church were required to have practiced what facet of hospitality?

   _____

   Explain what that means. _____

   _____

5. List some ways that a woman who works outside the home can still be hospitable and have the visiting preacher stay at her home. _____

   _____

   _____

Lesson 5

Hospitality with the Right Spirit

Hospitality as viewed in the scriptures stems from an attitude, not an ability to provide a sumptuous meal. In the *Layman's Bible Encyclopedia,* William Martin stated, "Hospitality is an act which depends for its effectiveness on the spirit in which it is performed." So, you see, it is not what we have to offer that matters; rather, it is how we share it. We find in John 4:24: "God is Spirit, and those who worship Him must worship in spirit and truth." So we can conclude that God looks at it as important. Let's examine what the scriptures say about the importance of our spirit in what we do.

We find that our spirit can take on God-like or sin-like attributes. Caleb was one of the spies Moses sent to scout the city of Jericho before the Israelites crossed the river to possess the promised land. The Bible tells us that "Caleb had a different spirit," because "he followed the Lord wholeheartedly" (Numbers 14:24).

We are also to have a spirit of humility. Psalm 34:18 says, "The Lord is near to those . . . and saves such as have a contrite [humble] spirit." God has always had a special place in His heart for those who are humble in their service to Him. In James 4:6 and 1 Peter 5:5 we read, "God resists the proud, but gives grace to the humble."

David prayed that God would "renew a steadfast spirit within me" (Psalm 51:10). When we see the word *renew,* we can conclude that he had this type of spirit at one time, but had lost it. We need to remember that God will renew our spirit if we keep His commandments and pray for His help. These are the attributes of the spirit God expects each of us to have and, like Caleb, we must follow Him whole-heartedly today.

Sadly, everyone doesn't have the kind of spirit that God wants him or her to have. In Proverbs 16:18 we find that a haughty spirit goes before a fall. Haughty is just the opposite of humble. Other terms used to describe this type of person are "puffed up," "arrogant," and "prideful." Remember, in Paul's great discourse on love, we find that godly love "is not puffed up" (1 Corinthians 13:4).

Another type of spirit not approved of God is stubborn-ness. We find that Pharaoh was stubborn (Exodus 13:15), the Israelites were stubborn (Deuteronomy 9:27), and Sihon (king of Heshbon) had a stubborn spirit (Deuteronomy 2:30). How does God look at stubbornness? In 1 Samuel 15:23 He says, "And stubbornness is as iniquity and idolatry." Would you want to be known to the Lord as an idolater?

"They began to make excuses."

There are numerous reasons why Christians don't practice hospitality as they should but, when examined closely, most of these reasons turn out to be excuses. Making excuses is not a new thing to the human race. In Luke 14:18 when the guests were told to come to the supper, we read, "But they all with one accord began to make excuses." When the host heard their reasoning, his attitude was, "For I say to you that none of those men who were invited shall taste my supper" (Luke 14:24). God didn't accept excuses then, and He won't accept them today. Don't get me wrong. I'm sure there are genuine reasons, occasionally, why someone cannot exercise this worthwhile service, but more often than not, these reasons won't hold water any more than a leaky bucket.

Let's examine, in light of the scriptures, some of the most common reasons that have been given.

"I'm too busy!"

Whether it is a job outside the home or responsibilities in the home, today's average Christian woman is stretched almost to her limits with demands on her time. After preparing meals, doing the laundry, cleaning the house, shuttling the children to various activities, studying the Bible, attending worship services—on and on we could go—there really isn't much time left for having guests in her home. We can all understand and sympathize with her.

There is an old expression that might be applicable in this situation: "Where there's a will there's a way." Many times we tend to use our responsibilities as an excuse not to do what someone else wants us to do. How many of us have not heard things like, "Mom, I can't wash the dishes if you want me to get my homework done!" Or, "I couldn't get my Bible class lesson completed; I'm in the band and we had a game Saturday night." You get the picture. If we really want to do something, we can work it in, one way or another.

One solution might be to get extra help from family members that day. Many foods, such as ham and potato salad, can be prepared ahead of time or even served cold. The answer might be as simple as just saying no the next time you're asked to volunteer for one of the many worthwhile causes that put a strain on your time. Many women get so wrapped up in other folks' problems that they might not leave enough time for the Lord or for the things that are necessary for their own spiritual growth.

"We don't have enough money to entertain."

I will be the first to admit that there are a lot of poor people in the world and in the Lord's church. Jesus said, "The poor you have with you always" (John 12:8). He left us an example to have compassion for their situation. Remember; it isn't what we have to share that matters to God, but how we share. Hospitality doesn't have to consist of a full meal, as many think, but can be much simpler. Just having someone in for a cup of coffee or a piece of cake can bring about beautiful and lasting relationships between people. We do not show hospitality to let folks know how much or how little we have, but to be together as a family and share our time with each other. After all, time is something we all have in common. However, someday, time will run out. Then our uppermost thought will be: "How have I used my time for God?"

"I'm not a people person."

I will not attempt to minimize this problem. I've met people who could not look you straight in the eye when they told you their name—people who had a real problem communicating with those around them. However, I've learned that even this can be overcome if the person really wants to do something about it.

One solution is to invite more than one person or one couple at a time. This lets the hostess off the hook when it comes to keeping a conversation going. It need not turn into a large dinner party, but the greater the number of people, the more conversation will flow. We knew a couple who was extremely hospitable, but the wife was very withdrawn and shy. She would call people on the phone to invite them, eliminating face-to-face contact, and then begin worrying about the planned evening. She would clean house all day the day before—even places no one would ever see— and fret for hours over what she was going to serve. When the day finally came, she would change clothes several times before settling on what she would wear. Then she would do something we sometimes forget. She would pray to God for the strength she needed to do what she knew she should do. She had faith in the passage which reads, "I can do all things through Christ, who strengthens me!" (Philippians 4:13). She would be nervous all through the meal, just knowing she had forgotten something important, but couldn't imagine what it was. When the evening was over she always said the same thing: "I'm glad we did it. This has really been good for me."

That's the key: Hospitality is not just for others. It is for me and my spiritual growth. I might add that this woman, by continuing her hospitable nature, overcame her unusual shyness and fear of people. Today she is a real asset to the congregation she attends, and her husband has all the qualifications to become a leader in the Lord's church.

"I'm single, and am hesitant to invite couples."

This is an understandable attitude, but it is an attitude that is only in the mind of the person. I've known many widows—and single folks, too—who opened their homes to guests and made them feel as welcome as any married couple could have. Several years ago when we lived in Florida, one of the most hospitable and godly women of the congregation was a victim of divorce. She held down a very stressful job with the city government. Rarely a Sunday evening went by that she didn't have several couples, as well as singles, into her home. She kept the menu simple— usually hotdogs and potato chips—but no one cared what she served. We just enjoyed getting together and encouraging one another. We all anxiously awaited the next time our turn would come to go to Gail Wright's home on Sunday night. Good memories and lasting friendships were made during those gatherings of brothers and sisters in Christ.

It is true that certain discretion should be practiced when you live alone. A single woman wouldn't want to invite only a man over for a meal, unless she is hoping for a closer relationship with him; however, she could invite a married couple along with him. I am acquainted with a preacher who married later in life. Up until the time he met his wife, he didn't let his being unmarried keep him from practicing hospitality. In fact, the women of the congregation got a real joy from watching him as he struggled with the problems of learning the fine arts of homemaking. I'm sure this helped him appreciate his future wife more fully than he would have had he never done any entertaining by himself.

"My husband does not like Christians in our house."

This may be true on rare occasions, but many times this is not absolutely true. It is often the believing wife who feels uncomfortable, and it usually falls into two categories of reasons.

The first category stems from the fact she is embarrassed by the fact her husband has no use for the church, and she's afraid of what he might say to her guests. Many times he really doesn't care who she invites, but he will, inevitably, do something that embarrasses his wife.

I heard of a woman's husband who offers her Christian friends a cold beer with their dinner, just to watch their reaction to his question or to see what they will say. This is childish behavior at best, and should be viewed as just that. But remember, this is his home, too, and according to God's law he is the head of it. His rudeness is his way of showing authority. There is an old expression; "To be forewarned is to be forearmed."

You might follow the example of a woman I know, who simply tells her guests ahead of time what they might encounter, and the problems are eliminated. There's no need to say anything in rebuttal to his statements or behavior. This is not the time to try to convert him to the Lord.

The second category is when she uses her unbelieving mate only as an excuse to get out of doing something she didn't want to do anyway. This is childish behavior on her part, and could result in a loss of her influence on her husband. Women in this situation are told that their unbelieving mates might "without the word, may be won by the conduct of their wives" (1 Peter 3:1).

"I'm ashamed of my house."

First let's establish why you are ashamed of your home. Is it too small? Is it in a state of poor repair? Is it not clean? Is it not as stylish as you'd like it to be? Some problems are within our power to change; others are not. When the reason for your feeling is isolated, then you can find a solution.

If the problem is cleanliness, grab a mop. While it is true that some women are better housekeepers than others, we can all do our best. If you are physically unable to do it yourself, ask for help. I knew an older Christian lady who loved to have company, but had reached a time in life when housecleaning was a burden to her. She solved the problem by asking some Christian friend to come the day before she was to have company and help her with the housework. I might add, she would include this friend in the guest list for the evening as a way of saying "thank you for your help."

If you feel your home isn't stylish enough, change it for the better. The public library has books and current magazines that show you ideas and directions for all kinds of decorating projects. If you feel inadequate in this field, ask a friend to help. Women who have a knack for this kind of thing really enjoy a chance to show off their talents. Depending on your finances, you can just rearrange what you already have or buy some new things. It really doesn't matter, as long as you like it.

If the problem is the state of repair, you can approach it from two different directions. If you have the ability to fix it up yourself, then you can begin. If you have the ability, but not the funds, or don't have the physical ability to do it yourself and don't have funds enough to hire it done, let someone know about it. There are many generous Christians who gladly donate their time, skills, and finances in helping their fellow brothers and sisters in the Lord. Many times, the problem is that those who need help have too much pride to ask for assistance. We in the church are a family, and we care about each other and want to help whenever we can. That is part of love! We must remember that hospitality is not about houses. It's about caring, sharing, fellowship, and growing closer together as time goes by.

"I am comfortable only with close friends."

Let's look at our perfect example again. Who did Jesus eat with when He walked on the earth? "And the Pharisees and scribes complained, saying, 'This Man receives sinners and eats with them'" (Luke 15:2). True, He didn't seek their company exclusively, but He did not exclude them from His guest list. While we may not identify with the term *publican* today, there are others who would fall into this same category. They would include the poor; the uneducated; those of another race; and those younger, older, wiser: the list goes on.

Do we tend to cull those we invite into our home? Are we ashamed to have "those kind" visit with us? How would the Lord look at our attitude? He said, "But if you love those who love you, what credit is that to you? For even sinners love those who love them" (Luke 6:32).

We should also practice hospitality without expecting anything in return. I've known people who counted visits. For example, I hear some say, "You had us over last, so it's our turn this time." This attitude hides the true purpose of hospitality, as it is taught in the scriptures. When Jesus was teaching about doing good to others, He said, "And if you lend to those from whom you hope to receive back, what credit is that to you? For even sinners lend to sinners to receive as much back" (Luke 6:34). This passage could easily be applied to the giving of hospitality to those who cannot repay our kindness, for one reason or another.

Practice Makes Perfect

How can I acquire this gift of being hospitable to others? I heard someone say that the best way to start something is to start. And how do you start? You start at the beginning and continue to grow. The book of Hebrews says, "Solid food belongs to those who are of full age, that is, those who by reason of use have their senses exercised [practiced] to discern both good and evil" (Hebrews 5:14). Practice is the key to becoming better at anything, whether physical or mental. God doesn't expect us to come into the church full grown, but He does expect growth. We are also admonished, "Therefore, leaving the discussion of the elementary principles of Christ, let us go on to perfection" (Hebrews 6:1). And further, "But above all these things put on love, which is the bond of perfection" (Colossians 3:14). Like all other attributes of Christianity, hospitality is one that will come easier to some than to others, but all of us must try. We are all different, but we are all important to the Lord. Remembering Romans 12:5–13 can help us with our attitudes toward those who might find accomplishing some things easier than we do.

We must keep the reason for doing what we do uppermost in our minds. The reason behind all our actions is love! Whenever we are afraid to try something—afraid of failure, afraid of what others might think, or just afraid— we need to remember what the Lord has told us: "There is no fear in love; but perfect love casts out fear, because fear involves torment. But he who fears has not been made perfect in love" (1 John 4:18).

Study Questions

1. According to the *Layman's Bible Encyclopedia,* hospitality is an act, which depends for its effectiveness on what? _____

    _____

2. What does it mean to worship God in Spirit? _____

    _____

3. What does it mean to worship God in truth? _____

    _____

4. What kind of spirit did Caleb have? _____
    Explain what this means. _____

    _____

5. What did David pray that God would renew in him?

    _____ _____

6. Of what kinds of spirits does God not approve?

    _____

7. When we take a closer look at the reasons people give for not following God's plan, what do we find they usually turn out to be?_____

    _____

8. What was the master's attitude toward those invited guests who made excuses as to why they could not attend his supper? _____

    _____

9. What does the Bible call "the bond of perfection"?

   _____

10. Romans 12:5–13 tells us that love is to be without what?

   _____

11. If we are afraid of trying to develop new talents, what passage will help our fear? _____

   Explain. _____

   _____

   _____

Lesson 6

BENEVOLENCE FROM THE BEGINNING

Benevolence, as defined in *Webster's Dictionary* is "an inclination to do good; kindliness; a kindly, charitable act or gift." As Christians, we are expected to be benevolent people. We will begin with the Old Testament and progress to what God expects of us today.

Israel and the Law Regarding the Poor
In giving the law to the Israelites at Mount Sinai, God left no area of their lives without guidance. Throughout history every society, from the developing nations to long-established governments, have had poor people. The Lord knew this—"For you have the poor with you always" (Matthew 26:11)—and made provision for them.

When the farmer gathered his crops, he was specifically told how to make allowances for the poor in his area.

> When you reap the harvest of your land, you shall not wholly reap the corners of your field, nor shall you gather the gleanings of your harvest. And you shall not glean your vineyard, nor shall you gather every grape of your vineyard; you shall leave them for the poor and the stranger: I am the Lord your God (Leviticus 19:9–10).

There are two areas covered in this passage: corners and gleanings.

- Corners: When they planted the field, they sowed the seed over the entire area. When they harvested, however, they were not to touch the corners of the field. That was to be reserved for the poor of the land and for the stranger—the traveler or foreigner. In Matthew 12:1; Mark 2:23; and Luke 6:1 we read the account of Jesus and His disciples becoming hungry on the Sabbath and taking advantage of this free food.

- Gleanings: The gleanings were those parts of the crop that were dropped or left behind by the reapers. The workers were not allowed to go back over the field again, but to leave that for the poor of the land. The great Moabitess, Ruth, gathered the dropped grain to feed herself and her mother-in-law, Naomi (Ruth 2:2–3). In fact, after she caught the eye of Boaz, who owned the field, he instructed the men to drop extra grain in her path.

In addition, as to how to plant and how to harvest, they were commanded to leave the land fallow every seventh year.

> Six years you shall sow your land and gather in its produce, but the seventh year you shall let it rest and lie fallow, that the poor of your people may eat; and what they leave, the beasts of the field may eat. In like manner you shall do with your vineyard and your olive grove (Exodus 23:10–11).

Since God's people could not harvest their crops on the seventh year, they had to make provision the previous year to store enough to carry them through. God does not forbid us to plan for the future by storing crops or by having a savings account at the bank. What He does forbid is stinginess with what we have and leaving Him out of our plans. The rich man (Luke 12:16–21) was not condemned for planning ahead. He was punished for being confident in himself, being stingy toward the misfortunate, and leaving God out of the process.

The Bible is full of instances of God's blessing those who love Him. He blessed the Israelites even when they rejected His commands. He was very specific, however, about their attitude toward the poor. Look at the scriptures below and you will understand how strongly He felt about the subject.

- Leviticus 19:15—"You shall not be partial to the poor, nor honor the person of the mighty."

- Deuteronomy 15:11—"For the poor will never cease from the land; therefore I command you, saying, You shall open your hand wide to your brother, to your poor and your needy, in your land."

- Zechariah 7:10—"Do not oppress the widow or the fatherless, the alien or the poor. Let none of you plan evil in his heart against his brother."

David and Solomon made several references to those who would not have a benevolent nature. David prayed that those who did not help the poor of the land would, as my uncle used to say, get their come-up-ence. David said in Psalm 10:2, "The wicked in his pride persecutes the poor; let them be caught in the plots which they have devised." A popular phrase we use today is, "What goes around, comes around."

Solomon knew that people are happier when they consider those living around them and try to help their neighbors with their needs. In Proverbs 14:21 we read, "He who despises his neighbor sins; but he who has mercy on the poor, happy is he." The word translated "despise" in this passage carries the idea of showing disrespect to others. Solomon calls this a sin. We know that sin will, sooner or later, cause unhappiness. Solomon also said that "the way of the transgressor is hard" (Proverbs 13:15).

Luke recorded the same idea in the words of Jesus in Acts 20:35: "It is more blessed to give than to receive." When you find a truly benevolent individual, one who gives without grumbling, you will find a happy person.

The wise man also said that when we neglect the poor, it is a reproach to God. "He who oppresses the poor reproaches his Maker, but he who honors Him has mercy on the needy" (Proverbs 14:31). The word *reproach* carries the idea of "to shame or discredit." When we neglect to do this work of righteousness, we fall into the same category as those mentioned in Hebrews 6:6: "They crucify again for themselves the Son of God, and put Him to an open shame."

Solomon states that when we help another person we are doing that service for our heavenly Father. He goes on to tell us that God will, in turn, reward us for these acts of kindness. "He who has pity on the poor lends to the Lord, and He will pay back what he has given" (Proverbs 19:17). Jesus taught the same lesson in Matthew 25:33–46. He condemned some of the people: "I was hungry and you gave Me no food; I was thirsty and you gave Me no drink." The people were shocked because they could not ever remember the Lord's being hungry or thirsty, and they certainly did not remember ever refusing to take care of His needs. Surely, they argued, He was mistaken in making this accusation. His reply was simple and to the point. "Assuredly, I say to you, inasmuch as you did not do it to one of the least of these, you did not do it to Me" (Matthew 25:45).

Failure to consider the poor will interfere with our prayers. Solomon said, "Whoever shuts his ears to the cry of the poor will also cry himself and not be heard" (Proverbs 21:13).

In Acts 10 we read the story of Cornelius. One of the things that got God's attention was this man's attitude toward the poor. In verse 10 we read: "Your prayers and your alms have come up for a memorial before God."

We, living under the New Testament, are commanded to add knowledge to our spiritual traits as we grow in our Christian life. "But also for this very reason, giving all diligence, add to your faith virtue, to virtue knowledge" (2 Peter 1:5). Knowledge, and the wisdom to apply that knowledge, does not all come from studying books. Much knowledge is gained by the experiences we have throughout life. It is a sad situation, indeed, when someone goes through an ordeal and learns nothing from it. As a rule, if a person doesn't learn a lesson the first time, it's doubtful he or she will the second time around. It's like the old saying: "No one learns a lesson the second time he is kicked by a mule."

Solomon describes the person who does not share his substance with the poor as a wicked individual, and one without knowledge. "The righteous considers the cause of the poor, but the wicked does not understand such knowledge" (Proverbs 29:7). Benevolence is like any other learned attribute: it gets better with practice. Hebrews 5:14 tells us: "But solid food belongs to those who are of full age, that is, those who by reason of use have their senses exercised to discern both good and evil." The more we practice benevolence, the more natural it will become.

Because King Nebuchadnezzar failed to recognize that his power came from God, he was driven into the wilderness where he remained for seven years. Daniel told him that he would again take the throne and that one way he could show that he had repented of his sins was to be benevolent toward the poor of the land.

> Therefore, O King, let my advice be acceptable to you; break off your sins by being righteous, and your iniquities

by showing mercy to the poor. Perhaps there may be a lengthening of your prosperity (Daniel 4:27).

The Virtuous Woman

In Proverbs 31 we meet the virtuous woman, and her many good qualities are listed. We are told that her worth is far above rubies. What did she do that was worth so much to the Lord and those with whom she came in contact? In verse 20 we see one quality that set her apart from other women. "She extends her hand to the poor, yes, she reaches out her hands to the needy." To reach out our hands does not always mean to give money, but it can encompass many things. If we as Christian women are to be worthy servants to our Maker, we must follow her example.

Study Questions

1. Define benevolence. _____

_____

2. What commands were the children of Israel given regarding the harvest of their crops? _____

_____

3. What did Boaz tell his hired help in regard to Ruth's gleaning in his fields? _____

_____

4. In Leviticus 19:9–10, what is meant by the term *stranger?* _____

_____

5. What was required of the Israelites regarding their farmland and vineyards every seven years? _____

_____

6. What fate did David wish for the man who "in his pride persecutes the poor"? _____

_____

7. What is the definition of the word *reproach?* _____

_____

8. He who oppresses the poor reproaches whom?

_____

9. When we help the poor to whom does the scriptures say we lend? _____

10. What will the Lord do in return? _____

_____

$\mathcal{L}$esson 7

WRITTEN FOR OUR LEARNING

The Bible has several examples of people who practiced benevolence toward those in need. Since we are told in Romans 15:4 "for whatever things were written before were written for our learning," let's see what lessons we can glean from these people of old. If we open our minds to their examples, they will do as Hebrews 11:4 says Adam and Eve's second son Abel does today: "He being dead still speaks."

Boaz

We meet Boaz for the first time in the second chapter of the book of Ruth. As you recall, Naomi had returned home to Bethlehem after living in the land of Moab for ten years. During that stay, she had lost her husband and both sons and was in a destitute condition. Feeling that she had nothing left to live for, she asked her name to be changed to Mara (Bitter) because she felt like the Lord had "dealt bitterly" with her.

Arriving home at the time of the barley harvest, Ruth went into the field of Boaz to glean behind the reapers. (Remember the previous lesson regarding the law of harvest?) Boaz noticed her and asked of his servant her identity.

After being told that she was Naomi's daughter-in-law, he instructed the men to drop extra grain in her path. He also fed her from his own table and told her not to go to any other field, but to stay in his fields during the entire harvest. Read Ruth 2:8–23 for this beautiful example of benevolence. It seems from verse 8 that Boaz was older than Ruth because he called her daughter. However, it is interesting to note that the Hebrew word translated here as "daughter" was also used to describe other relationships, both literally and figuratively. One translation of the word equates to our modern-day phrase, "apple of my eye."

The Good Samaritan

We meet this man in Luke 10:30–35 and are never told his name, only his nationality. The Jews took great pride in keeping their lineage pure, and they had no use for Gentiles. These Samaritans were not the original Jewish inhabitants of the land, but a displaced people. Let's briefly look at their background and you will understand why the Jews hated them so much.

In 2 Kings 17:23 we read about the nation of Israel being carried into captivity by the Assyrians. Assyria handled conquered people a bit different from the way the Babylonians did. (Babylon besieged Judah a few years later.) Assyria custom was to take the captives away from their homeland and replace them with captives from other countries. We read in 2 Kings 17:24:

> Then the king of Assyria brought people from Babylon, Cuthah, Ava, Hamath, and from Sepharvaim, and placed them in the cities of Samaria instead of the children of Israel; and they took possession of Samaria and dwelt in its cities.

Once this melting pot of races was established in Samaria, the people began to worship the gods of their homelands. Trouble ensued. The country became overrun with lions, and some of the people were killed. Somehow they knew Jehovah sent the lions because they were not worshiping Him. (Here's another example of God's expecting a Gentile nation to serve Him.) The king of Assyria sent an Israelite priest to Samaria to teach the people there how to worship God. Once they learned about Him, they began to worship Jehovah, but continued to worship their old gods as well. God stopped the lions, but the Samaritans continued to offer polluted worship to Him throughout their history. Now, back to the account of the good Samaritan.

In Luke 10:30 we read about a man who was traveling from Jerusalem to Jericho and was mugged on the way. Not only did the thieves take his money and clothing, but they also beat him so badly they thought he was dead.

Now picture an Israelite priest traveling along the same road and finding this misfortunate man. You would think if anybody would lend a hand it would be a priest. After all, he was a man of God and one who knew the law regarding showing mercy to other people. The scriptures tell us that "he passed by on the other side."

The next traveler we meet is a Levite. He followed the example of the priest and crossed to the other side of the road also.

In verse 33 we meet a Samaritan. Remember, the Jews looked down on the Samaritans and held them in contempt. In fact, they called them dogs. This Samaritan, however, had compassion on the injured man and stopped to lend aid. He did what he could at the scene and then took the wounded man to an inn for further care. He paid for that care out of his own pocket and promised to pay more if it was needed.

Compassion toward the unfortunate is the first step toward demonstrating the type of benevolence the Lord requires. As in all Christian characteristics, the heart must get right first if we are to be acceptable to God. Proverbs

23:7 tells us: "For as he thinks in his heart, so is he." What we need to realize is that when we show mercy to others, we receive blessings from that act as much as the person does to whom we show mercy. The poet said:

> The quality of mercy is not strained. It droppeth as the gentle rain from heaven upon the place beneath. It is twice blessed; it blesseth him that gives and him that takes (William Shakespeare in the *Merchant of Venice*).

Zacchaeus

In Luke 19 we meet the famous "wee little man" of whom children sing: Zacchaeus. He was a tax collector, a profession that was not too noble during the time of Christ. Verse 2 calls him a "chief tax collector," which usually indicated a person in a supervisory position. In other words, he would negotiate with the Roman government to be allowed to collect the taxes, but would turn around and hire others to actually do the collecting.

No matter what his status was in his chosen profession, he was a very benevolent man. This was out of character for a tax collector, because they usually compelled people to pay more taxes than they owed, and then pocketed the difference. In verse 8, however, Zacchaeus told the Lord: "Look, Lord, I give half of my goods to the poor; and if I have taken anything from anyone by false accusation, I restore four-fold." You couldn't want a more benevolent nature than that. Because of his godly nature, Jesus said this about him: "Today salvation has come to this house."

The Early Christians

When the church was established on Pentecost (Acts 2) there were many Jews in Jerusalem, who had traveled there for the feast days. When they heard the apostles preach and obeyed the gospel, they delayed their return home in order to learn more about Christianity. Consequently, their traveling money ran out, and many were doing without daily necessities. In Acts 2:44–45 we read: "Now all who believed were together, and had all things in common, and sold their possessions and goods, and divided them among all, as anyone had need." The same attitude is seen in Acts 4:32–37. These people were now part of the family of God and part of the body of Christ. They opened their hearts with compassion—there's that word again—for their fellow-Christians, and then they opened their purses to share with those in need. Their example has remained for almost two thousand years for us to see.

Will we ever have to sell what we have to share it with others? Probably not, but we should have the attitude that, if it were ever necessary we would not hesitate to do whatever we could to help someone in need.

Cornelius

Cornelius was a Gentile who prayed to Jehovah. We should not find this unusual, since God expected both Jews and Gentiles to worship Him. The means of worship was just different. The Israelites had been set aside as a special people through whom the Messiah would be born. They were given special laws and rituals to follow in worship to the Lord. The Gentiles continued to be under whatever law that had been in force before the Israelites became a special people, but that's another lesson for another time.

When we meet him in Acts 10, Cornelius is described as "a devout man and one who feared God with all his household, who gave alms generously to the people, and prayed to God always." God heard his prayers and noticed his benevolence toward his fellow men. How do we know this? In verse 4 the angel that had appeared to Cornelius told him, "Your prayers and your alms have come up for a memorial before God." God notices when we are compassionate toward the unfortunate, and these acts rise up as a memorial to Him.

Conclusion

What can we learn from all of these examples? We see without a doubt that God commands us to practice benevolence. How do we do that? The ways are as numerous as there are people on the earth. We just have to remember, as these people we have studied, that we belong to God; therefore, everything we have is His also. We read in Ezekiel 18:4: "Behold, all souls are Mine."

- Let us do like Boaz and leave handfuls for those in need.

- Let us do like the good Samaritan and make no difference in the kind of people we help.

- Let us practice what Zacchaeus did and always treat others fairly, not forgetting the poor.

- Let us be like the early Christians and realize that all we have is on loan from the Lord. Let us use it to the glory of His name.

- Let us be like Cornelius and have our prayers and alms rise as a memorial to God.

- Let us realize, in short, that it is as Jesus said, "The poor you have with you always" (John 12:8). Since this is the case, we need to spend our entire life perfecting this spiritual gift of benevolence.

Study Questions

1. Why were so many things written in the scriptures for us to read? _____

_____

2. What does Hebrews 11:4 tell us about Abel? _____

_____

3. What did Boaz instruct his workers to do in order to help Naomi and Ruth in their distress?

_____

4. Give a brief history of the Samaritan people.

_____

_____

_____

_____

5. What is the first step toward demonstrating the type of benevolence the Lord requires? _____

_____

6. Because of the benevolent nature of Zacchaeus, what did Jesus tell him had come to his house that day?

_____

7. What did the new Christians living in Jerusalem do for those who had traveled from other places and came to need assistance? _____

_____

8. Before Christ came, to what law was Cornelius (and other Gentiles) accountable? _____

_____

9. What two things from Cornelius had gone up as a memorial to God? _____

_____

10. All of what did the Lord say was His? _____

_____

11. Whom did Jesus say we would have with us always?

_____

Lesson 8

BENEVOLENCE AND ME

Okay. We know God's people in the scriptures were benevolent toward others. We understand we are to be benevolent if we are to please the Lord. But how? How can I take the examples and commands in the Bible and apply them to me . . . today . . . in my present circumstances?

Benevolence, in its simplest form, simply means to give. Giving, however, is against human nature. From the cradle children know how to take, but giving is something that must be learned. Paul tells us, "When I was a child, I spoke as a child, I understood as a child, I thought as a child; but when I became a man, I put away childish things" (1 Corinthians 13:11).

Attitude

First, let's look at attitude. This is just another way of saying, prepare your heart. Second Corinthians 8:12 says, "For if there is first a willing mind, it is accepted according to what one has, and not according to what he does not have." Matthew 12:35 goes on to say, "A good man out of the good treasure of his heart brings forth good things, and an evil man out of the evil treasure brings forth evil things." The kind of mind-set we have will determine if we will give and serve others as we are supposed to give. Philippians 2:4–5 tells us, "Let each of you look out not only for his own interests, but also for the interests of others. Let this mind be in you which was also in Christ Jesus."

Sports teams have always known that the coach plays a big role in whether a team wins or loses. Is this because that person knows so much more about the game than the players know? Hardly! It is because he is a professional at giving the team a winning attitude. When players go into a game with the idea that they are winners and that they can accomplish their goals, they are much more likely to win than the team that approaches the game with a ho-hum attitude.

This same principle applies to Christianity. If we approach our giving—whether in worship or in our daily walk of life—with less than a hundred percent desire to do God's bidding, it will affect whether we possess that biblical benevolence that all Christians must have to please the Lord.

When we think of giving, money always comes to mind first, and this causes many people to display a defensive attitude. While money is certainly involved, benevolence includes so many more things. Let's examine just a few of these items.

Service

The scriptures tell us the Jesus "did not come to be served, but to serve" (Matthew 20:28). On one occasion He wrapped a towel around Himself and washed the feet of his followers (John 13:5). We, like Christ, were put on this earth to serve each other. After washing their feet, the Lord went on to say,

> If I then, your Lord and Teacher, have washed your feet, you also ought to wash one another's feet. For I have given

you an example, that you should do as I have done to you (John 13:14).

Does this mean that we should carry a basin of water around with us to wash everyone's feet? No. It means that we should be ready—and willing—to serve each others in whatever capacity is necessary.

I read a story a long time ago that's stuck with me for years. It seems that a woman had lost her father and, since he had lived in another state, she needed to prepare the family for a long car trip. Different ones called to offer sympathy and ended the conversation with the all too familiar phrase, "Now, if there's anything I can do, just call me." One man, however, used a different approach.

The doorbell rang and, when the woman answered, it was an elderly man from their congregation. He was armed with a cardboard box that contained a variety of shoe polish, rags, and brushes. "I've come to polish your shoes," he announced. "If you'll just gather up your family's shoes I'll take it from there."

The woman didn't know quite what to think but complied with the old gentleman's request. He took all the shoes out on the back porch, and the woman returned to her duties. She was so busy she forgot all about the man for a couple of hours. She headed to the back porch to apologize for her neglect. When she opened the door, the man was nowhere in sight. What she did see brought tears to her eyes. There, all in neat rows, were their shoes. Every bit of dirt had been brushed and cleaned away. Every scuff-mark was now covered with a fresh coat of polish. On top of the shoes was a small sheet of paper with the words: "God bless your family on your journey, and may He bring you safely home."

At the funeral the mother looked down at the feet of her children, all shod with shining shoes, and realized what this caring individual had done. "Such a small service," some people might say, but she understood differently. The old man seemed to know she would be so busy with preparations that this detail would probably not be done.

What lesson can we learn from this story? The next time someone is going through a hard time with sickness, death, or some other problem, don't just say, "If I can do anything call." Do like this gentleman did; find something you could do, then offer to do it. Here are some guidelines to get you started:

- Don't say: "Can I fix some food for your family?"

  Do say: "I've fixed a casserole for your family. When would be a good time to bring it by your house?"

- Don't say: "Can I help you pack for the trip?"

  Do say: "I know how dirty clothes can pile up when you are _____ [whatever the problem]. I'll come by in about thirty minutes to pick up your laundry. I'll take it home, wash it, and have it back to you this afternoon."

- Don't say: "I'm sorry you are so tired."

  Do say: "I know how tired you get when you're not feeling well. Would you please let me come by and pick up the children so you can get some rest? I'll take care of feeding them dinner and getting their baths and then bring them home about bedtime."

I'm sure you get the idea. Don't put the burden on the person needing the service to tell you what she needs. For a variety of reasons, most people will not do that. Jesus did not ask the disciples, "Hey guys, do you want me to wash your feet?" He knew what was needed and set about doing it. We should follow His example of service to others.

Time

Oh my! This commodity is something that we never seem to have enough to share with others, yet it is so needed in the church. Many times it is so much easier to drop some money into a hat, or donate some old clothes to a good cause, than it is to take time out of our busy schedule and give it to someone else. Giving of our time, however, is a benevolent act, and Christians must willingly share their time with those in need of it.

In Ephesians 5:15–16 we are told, "See then that you walk circumspectly, not as fools but as wise, redeeming the time, because the days are evil." Nearly the same words are used in Colossians 4:5, but the apostle is speaking of our interaction with non-Christians. "Walk in wisdom toward those who are outside, redeeming the time." The Greek word *exagorazo,* translated in both these passages as "redeeming," means "to buy up, ransom, or rescue from loss." In other words, how we use our time on earth will directly affect our salvation in heaven. That puts a whole new perspective on the topic of time. What kinds of people need my time?

The Lonely

Loneliness is said to be a curse of the elderly, but that is not true. Loneliness strikes every age and every class of people. In fact, according to several articles I've read, the more wealth and fame some people acquire, the lonelier they become. What's the cure? You are!

This is an area in our lives that we can help, and it won't cost a penny. Most people who are lonesome just want someone to drop by and talk. Who are these lonely people?

The elderly man or woman who is not sick but just stuck in the house alone most of the time. Look through photo albums and share memories with them. Take some busy work, like sewing on buttons or mending your children's clothes, to an elderly sister's home and tackle it while visiting. Watch for magazine or newspaper articles that might be of interest to some older friend. Since many of them have a problem seeing small print, offer to read the article to them while you are there.

Ask them if they would like to go to the grocery store, pharmacy, or some other place. If there's not a particular errand that needs running, they would probably enjoy just going for a drive.

One thing many older people don't get to do as often as they would like is to visit the grave of a loved one. To some folks this might sound morbid, but to many it is a helpful experience as they struggle to cope with life. A wife who loses a husband of many years, cannot just cut off the need to be with him.

A hint here: Have some small pruning tools in your car in case the grave needs attention. Pulling weeds or trimming tall grass with shears will endear you to a person for life. If your friend is physically able, she would probably enjoy sharing in the chore.

Use your imagination. It really doesn't matter what you do as you try to serve the lonely. Just caring enough to be there is a big help.

- A mother of small children, especially a single mother, often needs your visit. Most young mothers are starved for adult conversation. Take a magazine that demonstrates the latest fashions, gardening ideas, decorating, and recipes. You get the idea. The goal here is to let the individual know she is still an adult with whom spending time is worthwhile.

- Nursing homes are filled with lonely people, and not all of them are senile or unaware of what's going on around them. They long for someone—anyone—to drop by and make the dreary day shorter. Take your children; take your pet. (Check with the management on this one.) They enjoy everyday things that we take for granted.

Shut-ins live a very confined life, and you can be that ray of sunshine that makes a day special.

- Some children, believe it or not, lead a very lonely existence. They go to school and come home to an empty house. Many parents are so busy making a living that they do not think to give their children what they need the most—their time. Offer to have a couple of little girls come to your house for an afternoon. Better yet, set up a schedule so they can come on a regular basis. Do things that mothers usually do, like baking cookies, going shopping, or working on a craft together. The influence you have over young lives cannot be measured. It is time well spent.

Take note of one very important thing: Whatever you do, do not criticize the child's parents for not spending time with her. If the child does, you might say something like this: "I'm sorry your mom's so busy. I'm sure she loves you very much and wants you to have nice things."

Those in Need

We all know people who are in need. Sometimes they need more than we can financially give, but we must do what we can. For those of us who can sew, we can make clothes for someone who needs them. If you can't sew, then thrift stores and garage sales have treasures for the finding. If you purchase items at one of these places, be sure to wash and iron them before giving them away.

We read of a sister in the church at Joppa. She became sick and died. The disciples sent to Lydda and begged Peter to come. When he got there, "all the widows stood by him weeping, showing the tunics and garments which Dorcas had made while she was with them" (Acts 9:39). Dorcas had used her talent for sewing to make garments for the widows in the community. After her death, it was these items that brought her memory before her friends. Peter had compassion and raised her from the dead. Can't you just imagine what a blessing this was on all those people to whom she was so benevolent?

This type of benevolence is looked at as important to the Lord. We are told in the first chapter of James that our religion is useless without it. He goes on in verse 27 to say, "Pure and undefiled religion before God and the Father is this: to visit orphans and widows in their trouble, and to keep oneself unspotted from the world." To visit "in their trouble" does not mean to make note of it and do nothing. This carries the idea that we are to do whatever we can to alleviate their trouble. True, we don't all have the money to pay other's bills, but we must do whatever is in our ability to accomplish.

While single mothers are not classed technically as widows in our society, they come really close. Think about it. Many may be divorced and raising their children without any help from an ex-husband. It is so easy to become discouraged in a situation like this. Trying to hold down a job and be both mother and father is an almost impossible task. As Christian women, we must help to fill that gap and "strengthen the weak hands, and make firm the feeble knees. Say to those who are fearful-hearted, 'Be strong, do not fear!'" (Isaiah 35:3–4).

Conclusion

When we are not benevolent and do not give as we should, we rob God. You say you would never rob the Lord? Well, the people in Malachi's day said the same thing, and God issued a challenge to them.

> Will a man rob God? Yet you have robbed Me! But you say, In what way have we robbed You? In tithes and offerings. You are cursed with a curse, for you have robbed Me, even this whole nation. Bring all the tithes into the

storehouse, that there may be food in My house. And try Me now in this, says the Lord of hosts, if I will not open for you the windows of heaven and pour out for you such blessing that there will not be room enough to receive it (Malachi 3:8–10).

You cannot out-give the Lord! Trust me on this one because I've tried it. It works! I could tell you story after story about someone who gave to the church, or to someone in need, and the blessings came back multiplied many times. In this passage, God is coming as close to a wager as you will ever see. He dares us to give to the church and to those in need first—then we are to sit back and watch the blessings roll in.

Study Questions

1. Benevolence in its simplest form means what? _____

   _____

2. When someone needs to work on his or her attitude, what does that involve? _____

   _____

3. We are to look out after our own interests, but also the interest of whom else?

   _____

4. What is one of the main duties of a coach? _____

   _____

5. What are two things besides money that constitute benevolence? _____

   _____

6. We are told to walk wisely, redeeming the time, because the days are what? _____

7. What is the meaning of the word that's translated "redeeming" in both Ephesians 5:15 and Colossians 4:5? _____

_____

8. What is said to be a curse of the elderly? _____

_____

9. What are the two names of the benevolent person in Acts 9 who used her talent for sewing to help others?

_____

10. What is described as "pure religion" in the scriptures?

_____

Lesson 9

Does God Require Us to Teach Others?

Evangelism is from a Greek word meaning "gospel" or "good news." When we add the verb "to bring" we get the phrase that is usually translated "preach." According to G. William Schweer in the *Holman Bible Dictionary,* evangelism is "the active calling of people to respond to the message of grace and commit oneself to God in Jesus Christ."

Evangelism is not a duty that is restricted to the New Testament. God has always expected His people to be active in sharing His teaching with others. He instructed the Israelites to begin their ministry with their own family. In Deuteronomy 11:18–20, He told them:

> Therefore you shall lay up these words of mine in your heart and in your soul, and bind them as a sign on your hand, and they shall be as frontlets between your eyes. You shall teach them to your children, speaking of them when you sit in your house, when you walk by the way, when you lie down, and when you rise up. And you shall write them on the doorposts of your house and on your gates.

There were two ways evangelism was accomplished during the time of the law of Moses. The first was to make proselytes of the people they met. This simply meant a non-

Jew agreed to adopt the Jewish religion as their own and to follow the laws God gave to Moses on Mount Sinai. We see this kind of conversion in Ruth 1:16, when Ruth told Naomi,

> Entreat me not to leave you, or to turn back from following after you; for wherever you go, I will go; and wherever you lodge, I will lodge; your people shall be my people, and your God, my God.

Ruth traveled to Palestine with her mother-in-law and became faithful in keeping all the ordinances of the law, even though she was a Gentile by birth.

The other type of evangelism we see in the Old Testament was God expecting Gentiles to turn from their idolatry and worship Him. One case in point was His directions to the prophet Jonah when He commanded him to "arise, go to Nineveh, that great city [a Gentile city], and preach to it the message that I tell you" (Jonah 3:2). Jonah had decided that it would do no good to preach to "those wicked people," but God can see when man is blinded by his own prejudices. We find in Jonah 3:8 that after hearing the words of the Lord, the king made this proclamation: "But let man and beast be covered with sackcloth, and cry mightily to God; yes, let every one turn from his evil way and from the violence that is in his hands." These people did not become subject to the law of Moses. They did not have to keep the Passover, offer sacrifices in Jerusalem, or become members of one of the twelve tribes of Israel. God expected them to turn from the worship of false gods and begin worshiping Him, the one and only true God.

In the New Testament, the law we are under today, God's evangelical message is the same for everyone—Jew and Gentile alike. Isaiah prophesied about the coming of the church and that the gospel would be spread "going forth out of Jerusalem" (Isaiah 2:2–4). This, of course, is referring to the establishment of the church (Acts 2). Today we are told, "There is neither Jew nor Greek, there is neither slave nor free, there is neither male nor female; for you are all one in Christ Jesus" (Galatians 3:28). We also note in Acts 17:30: "Truly, these times of ignorance God overlooked, but now commands all men everywhere to repent."

Our Success Depends on Our Attitude

Before we can begin to teach others we must examine our own feelings. We must incorporate two things into our lives: love for the sinner and hatred of sin. We are told in Romans 5:8 that "while we were sinners Christ died for us"—this means me! His death on the cross was the ultimate gift of love one person can give another (John 15:13). Jesus truly loved the people He came to serve. We find that He had compassion for them because of their lost condition. In Matthew 9:36 we read: "But when He saw the multitudes, He was moved with compassion for them, because they were weary and scattered, like sheep having no shepherd." Jesus became that good shepherd (John 10:11, 14). Since Christ is our ultimate example, we should love those around us, have compassion on them, and try to follow His instructions to Peter, "Feed my sheep" (John 21:17).

Even though Jesus loved the scattered sheep, He hated the sin that was causing their destruction. "The way of the wicked is an abomination to the Lord" (Proverbs 15:9); "You have loved righteousness and hated lawlessness" (Hebrews 1:9). We, too, are admonished to follow His example in this. We must hate sin and be moved to try to save those who are corrupted by it.

> But you, beloved, building yourselves up on your most holy faith, praying in the Holy Spirit, keep yourselves in the love of God, looking for the mercy of our Lord Jesus Christ unto eternal life. And on some have compassion, making a distinction; but others save with fear, pulling

them out of the fire, hating even the garment defiled by
the flesh (Jude 20–23).

The story is told of a tour bus traveling through a slum
area of a large city. The tourists noticed a small girl playing
in the gutter. She was dressed in rags and was very, very
dirty. A passenger on the bus remarked, "That has got to be
the filthiest child I've ever seen. Why doesn't her mother
clean her up? Doesn't she love her?"

The tour guide answered, "That little girl's mother
probably loves her very much; she just doesn't mind the
dirt. You hate the dirt but you don't love her enough to
clean her up. Until the love of the person and the hate of
the dirt are in the same individual's heart, that child will
probably remain dirty."

Can you see the spiritual application here? We must
love everyone if we are to please God, and we must equally
hate sin and what it has done to the people with whom we
come in contact. In 1 John 3:18 we read, "My little children,
let us not love in word or in tongue, but in deed and in
truth." This is another example of the Bible using the word
love as a verb.

How Do We Teach?

We teach two ways: by verbal instructions and by
example. Paul said of his preaching: "For I will not dare to
speak of any of those things which Christ has not accomplished through me, in word and deed, to make the Gentiles
obedient" (Romans 15:18). Again, we read in Colossians 3:17:
"And whatever you do in word or deed, do all in the name of
the Lord Jesus, giving thanks to God the Father through
Him." Let's talk about our example first.

Early in His ministry Jesus taught the importance for
His followers to set the right example in this world. In
Matthew 5:16 He said, "Let your light so shine before men,
that they may see your good works and glorify your Father

in heaven." In the same chapter, in verse 13, He tells His disciples: "You are the salt of the earth." In Philippians 2:15 we are told why we should shine like lights "that you may become blameless and harmless, children of God without fault in the midst of a crooked and perverse generation, among whom you shine as lights in the world." The church in Thessalonica turned to God with such fervor that Paul told them:

> You became examples to all in Macedonia and Achaia who believe. For from you the word of the Lord has sounded forth, not only in Macedonia and Achaia, but also in every place. Your faith toward God has gone out, so that we do not need to say anything (1 Thessalonians 1:7–8).

Wouldn't it be wonderful if all Christians lived like those people, so that their lives would proclaim Christ even without saying a word?

In 1 Peter 3:1–2, the apostle addresses the problem of a Christian's being married to an unbeliever when he tells those wives that their husbands "without the word, may be won by the conduct of their wives, when they observe your chaste conduct accompanied by fear." We must understand, however, that this is not an absolute. The scripture says, "May be won." The final decision still rests with the individual, but the believer's good example greatly increases the odds for success.

How can a wife ever hope to convert her husband if she doesn't strictly follow God's law? We are told to "rejoice in the truth" (1 Corinthians 13:6). If he sees her less than a hundred percent truthful, how can he believe her teachings from the scriptures? We are told to "do all things without complaining and disputing" (Philippians 2:14), so how can he respect her beliefs about God if she has a reputation for nagging and complaining. Wives are told to "submit to your own husbands, as is fitting in the Lord" (Colossians 3:18). Notice that the passage does not add "if he is a Christian." God placed this guideline in marriage for all people; He expects it to be followed. True, her allegiance to God comes first. In matters that do not restrict her service to the Lord, however, she is to be in subjection to her chosen mate. If a Christian wife rebels against her husband's authority, how can she convince him that a life of dedication to the Lord is important to her? Hard to do, you say? Yes, but we must bear the consequences of our choices on this earth. This is one reason it is so important to take extra care and plenty of time in selecting a life-long companion.

Study Questions

1. What does the word *evangelism* mean? _____

_____

2. What two types of evangelism do we find taking place in the Old Testament? _____

_____

3. Give an example of a specific Jewish proselyte found in the scriptures. _____

_____

4. Give a Bible example of Gentiles turning to Jehovah.

_____

5. How many evangelical messages from God do we have today? _____

6. What two things must we make a part of our attitudes if we are to be successful at teaching others about the Lord? _____

    _____

7. Why did Jesus have compassion for the multitudes that followed Him? _____

    _____

8. We are taught to "have compassion" on others because of their lost condition, "save them with fear," and to hate what? _____

9. In what two ways do we teach others about God?

    _____

    _____

10. Drawing from your own observations, list some suggestions that a wife might use to help convince her husband, or her children, of the importance of Christianity? _____

    _____

    _____

    _____

    _____

    _____

11. Ultimately, whose responsibility is it to obey the Lord's commands? _____

    _____

Lesson 10

How Can I Be Successful
at Evangelism?

The Joy of Salvation

Before anyone can be truly successful at anything, he or she must have the desire to succeed. Do you find yourself wanting to talk about spiritual things, or are you a little embarrassed when the conversation turns religious? We should enjoy the prospect of sharing our love for the Lord with others. Until we do this we cannot convey to them the peace that is beyond understanding that Christians possess (Philippians 4:7). David said, "Restore to me the joy of Your salvation . . . Then I will teach transgressors Your ways, and sinners shall be converted to You" (Psalm 51:12–13). Until the joy is there, God's work will go lacking. This joy of which David spoke gives us strength from God. Nehemiah said, "The joy of the Lord is your strength" (Nehemiah 8:10). In the New Testament we find that joy is a part of the Christian's spiritual fruit: "But the fruit of the Spirit is love, joy, peace, long-suffering, kindness, goodness, faithfulness (Galatians 5:22).

We might add that God will hold us accountable if we do not have this joy of His salvation in our lives. In Deuteronomy 28:45–47 He told the people:

> Moreover all these curses shall come upon you and pursue and overtake you, until you are destroyed, because . . . you did not serve the Lord your God with joy and gladness of heart.

We must be on guard lest we find ourselves in the same condition as the children of Israel were in Lamentations 5:15: "The joy of our heart has ceased." Instead, let us get on with the reason we are on this earth in the first place: doing our Father's business. If a person has that desire, then "God keeps him busy with the joy of his heart" (Ecclesiastes 5:20). How much fruit the gospel yields depends on the hearts of those who are taught (Mark 4:3–8). The Lord has promised that His word will not return void, but He depends on us to share it joyfully with others (Isaiah 55:12).

Who can I teach?

One good place to start is with the equation found in Matthew 7:7—Ask + Seek = Find

When we go shopping for something we really want, we will look everywhere for it. If we don't find it, we ask a store employee where it is. Why don't we apply this same principle to finding people to teach about the Lord? Sadly, many times we tend to put more effort into finding the right pair of shoes to wear to a special event than we do in fulfilling our roles in the Lord's business.

The number of prospects we can find to teach is limited only by our own imagination and determination. Coworkers, neighbors, employees where we shop, the person who mows our lawn, our hairdresser, our mail carrier, and our children's teachers are all prospects—the list goes on and on. There is no shortage of people we can talk to about our faith; we just have to get up and get going.

The first rule of evangelism is, do not cull anyone. We tend to be a bit prejudiced in our search for Christian candidates, but this is not God's idea of spreading the gospel.

Think about some of the followers of Christ in the New Testament whom we would have probably passed over when it came to using our time trying to convert them. What about Matthew, a customs agent (Matthew 9:9); Zacchaeus, a chief tax collector (Luke 19:5); Paul, a murderer of Christians and a hater of Jesus (Acts 8:3); Mary Magdalene, a woman out of whom Jesus had cast seven demons (Mark 16:9); Simon of Bethany—Hey! He had leprosy! (Matthew 26:6). In addition, there is a list in 1 Corinthians 6:9–10 that reads: "Fornicators, idolaters, adulterers, homosexuals, sodomites, thieves, covetous, drunkards, revilers, extortioners." A list of depraved and lost souls, you ask? No! These are the former characteristics of the Christians that made up the church at Corinth. We must remember that the "soap" of the gospel can clean all sin from anyone who obeys the Lord's commandments for attaining salvation.

Friendliness Pays Off

When you come together in the assembly, speak to as many people as you can. Make it a point not to get into the habit of talking to the same few folks week after week. Try to have a conversation with a different person after each service. Notice, I didn't say "speak" but "have a conversation." When you converse with someone it should go beyond, "How do you do?" Just before worship is the time to get to know our spiritual family a little better. It is also a time to meet visitors. Be sure to get their names, addresses, and phone numbers. Visitors indicate their interest by their presence, and since they are interested, we want them to know we are interested in them also. In fact, we should be interested enough to call them or go to their home and see if we can be of service.

Some very good prospects are unbelieving mates and children of the members in our own congregation. The first step is to get to know these people on a social basis, then try to reach them with the gospel. I have been in congregations where members who have attended for years didn't even know that a certain fellow Christian in the church had a living spouse, simply because the spouse had never been to an assembly. Can you imagine having a physical brother or sister and not even knowing if he or she were married or not? These folks, who may be the lone light in their family, have an extra burden to carry and we, as part of their spiritual family, must follow Paul's admonishment to "bear one another's burdens" (Galatians 6:2).

If you have already done what you could with your own neighbors and friends, ask another church member to suggest a contact for a home Bible study. Have that fellow Christian invite you and the prospect for coffee so you won't be strangers when you later propose a Bible study. It is always easier to talk with someone you've met than to talk with someone you do not know at all.

"Housebound" Does Not Mean "Hands Bound"

"I can't drive and get around, so I can't take the gospel outside of my home," someone might say. Being homebound does place certain restrictions on evangelism, but it doesn't free you from responsibility. You are not necessarily restricted to those who might come to visit you.

The telephone can be used as a tool to reach out and touch someone with the gospel. There is always a need to check on those who were absent from the regular assembly, discouraged from life's problems, or spiritually sick. We cannot all be medical doctors and cure diseases, but being a listening and caring friend can cure many problems that cause heavy hearts. If someone's needs are beyond your capabilities, you can pass the information on to another who would be able to take care of it.

Sending cards and letters is an excellent way to reach souls who need encouragement or teaching. The key is not to let confinement become a disability or an excuse that hinders you from using whatever ability you have in furthering the cause of the Lord, even if it is only one small talent. There are many good Bible correspondence courses available. Sending these to folks you know is a good way to teach the gospel without ever having to leave your easy chair.

Charity—and Evangelism—Begins at Home

We must not overlook those of our own family. Almost all members of the church have a relative who is not a Christian, or one who has fallen away. The excuse, "I don't want to push them," has been overdone to the point of neglect. True, you must use a special kind of tact and consideration when approaching a relative, but the key idea that should shine predominately in your association is, "I care about you and your soul." The problem comes when those we attempt to teach sense an argumentative attitude instead of a genuine love for their well being. This goes back to the idea we have talked about in the past: hate sin but love sinners enough to want to help them escape from the error of their way. Over the years, I've heard so many unbelieving mates of Christians say that the reason they never obeyed the gospel was because of the attitude of the person trying to teach them. Nagging, belittling, and arguing will not help us accomplish the mission God has for us.

The scriptures are full of warnings about the problems of being contentious. The wise man Solomon made many observations about contention:

- "A brother offended is harder to win than a strong city, and contentions are like the bars of a castle" (Proverbs 18:19).

- "Better to dwell in a corner of a housetop, than in a house shared with a contentious woman" (Proverbs 21:9).

- "Better to dwell in the wilderness, than with a contentious and angry woman" (Proverbs 21:19).

- "It is better to dwell in a corner of a housetop, than in a house shared with a contentious woman" (Proverbs 25:24).

- "A continual dripping on a very rainy day and a contentious woman are alike" (Proverbs 27:15).

Paul spoke of contention in 1 Corinthians 11:16 when he said, "But if anyone seems to be contentious, we have no such custom, nor do the churches of God." We can safely conclude then that arguing and other such behavior cannot be a part of a Christian's life. Timothy was admonished to "avoid foolish and ignorant disputes, knowing that they generate strife" (2 Timothy 2:23). Contention is listed as one of the works of the flesh in Galatians 5:20, along with idolatry, sorcery, hatred, jealousies, outbursts of wrath, selfish ambitions, dissensions, and heresies. As Christian women, we certainly do not want our names to be on this list.

One thing we don't want to leave out of this study is the importance of our being willing to teach a children's Bible class. Children are not born with spiritual knowledge or an understanding of the will of God. The Lord has left us in charge of their teaching and guidance, and we will be held accountable if we fall short in this duty. He told His disciples: "Let the little children come to Me, and do not forbid them; for of such is the kingdom of heaven" (Matthew 19:14). If they are not taught, they may soon lose faith in the Lord and turn away from Him. Jesus voiced His feelings on this when He said,

> But whoever causes one of these little ones who believe in Me to stumble, it would be better for him if a millstone were hung around his neck, and he were thrown into the sea (Mark 9:42).

While it is true that some women do not have the ability to teach, this is the exception, not the rule. It has been my experience that most of the reasons women give for not teaching are the same as those in Luke 14:18: "But they all with one accord began to make excuses." God's attitude toward them was that "none of them will taste My supper." Is this what we want the Lord to tell us when we arrive for that great supper in heaven? If you don't know how to teach, then learn. God expects us to develop as Christians, to grow "in the grace and knowledge of our Lord and Savior Jesus Christ. To Him be the glory both now and forever. Amen" (2 Peter 3:18).

One of the church's greatest sources of wisdom is that of the older women, yet most of them, when asked to teach, reply: "I did that for years; it's someone else's turn now," or "I'm retired, let the younger ones do that." I understand that bad nerves can go with aging and that children tend to bother us more as we grow older. However, this is also the exception to the rule. Most women love being around their grandchildren. What is the difference? If you feel you can't handle the class by yourself, ask a younger Christian to help. Then your assistant will gain wisdom by sitting at the feet of a mature Christian and will learn the importance of teaching the church of tomorrow.

What If They Won't Listen?

Jesus said we are sowers of the seed, and we cannot be responsible for the soil the seed falls upon. This doesn't make it easier to handle the disappointment when someone we want to reach turns his or her back on God's commandments. We teach with tears and prayers, but we also have to understand that the decision rests with each individual. We can only do our part, which is sharing what we know about the will of the Lord.

The fear of being rejected causes many to shy away from trying to take the gospel to their friends, neighbors, and family. We can't let this kind of feeling take over our minds. Everyone will not heed the call; everyone will not care what the Lord expects them to do; everyone will not listen when you try to show them the way to true happiness, but God hears you, and He has said that we should be "faithful until death, and I will give you the crown of life" (Revelation 2:10).

When Christ walked the earth, not everyone listened to Him either. This broke His heart and caused Him great sadness. On one occasion He said,

> O Jerusalem, Jerusalem, the one who kills the prophets and stones those who are sent to her! How often I wanted to gather your children together, as a hen gathers her chicks under her wings, but you were not willing! (Matthew 23:37).

Many will say no to the Lord's invitation, but we cannot let that keep us from trying to lead others to Christ. How much is one soul worth? How much would you give if you could buy your way into heaven? We cannot afford to be weary in well doing because we know God lives and that He is able to do all that He has promised. We can partake of these promises if we will do our part. The purpose of our learning and teaching is to pass our knowledge along through those we teach who will, in turn, teach others. This is the way God's kingdom is perpetuated from generation to generation. "And the things that you have heard from me among many witnesses, commit these to faithful men who will be able to teach others also" (2 Timothy 2:2). It has been said that "evangelism is not finished until the evangelized becomes the evangelist."

"Sounds like work," you say? Well, how much work is too much to avoid an eternity without God? Remember the words of the song, "Heaven will surely be worth it all."

Study Questions

1. What is the first rule of evangelism? _____

_____

2. List the kinds of people the Corinthian Christians were before they obeyed the gospel? _____

_____

3. How much interest should we show in the visitors to our assembly? _____

_____

4. Name one reason an unbelieving mate might never be interested in the church. _____

_____

5. What did Paul tell Timothy that foolish arguments caused? _____

_____ _____

6. List the works of the flesh. _____

_____

_____

7. What mathematical equation can we use in finding prospects to teach? _____

8. If someone doesn't know how to teach a class, list some things she can do about the problem?

_____

_____

_____

_____

9. To whom will the Lord give a crown of life? _____

_____

10. Explain the meaning of Matthew 23:37. _____

_____

_____

11. In addition to saving the souls of other people, why is it important that we teach the gospel?

_____

12. It is said that evangelism is not finished until what?

_____

13. According to Philippians 4:4, 7, when will a Christian have the peace of God, which surpasses all understanding? _____

_____

14. According to Isaiah 55:10–11, with what does God compare spreading His word? _____

_____

Lesson 11

LET'S START WITH A GOOD FOUNDATION

If someone is going to begin a career as a teacher, there is a certain amount of training that must go on first. A person who knows only basic arithmetic—addition and subtraction—could, conceivably, teach math. However, the instruction is much more effective if the teacher has studied all forms of math—algebra, geometry, and calculus. If a woman knew only how to sew a straight seam and make only one garment, she could, in a limited fashion, teach someone else to sew. However, she would be a more credible instructor if she knew something about fitting, fabric, and the like.

The same principle holds true for teaching the Bible. The more we study and learn, the more effective workers we can be for the Lord. Does this mean we are to wait until we know it all to begin obeying God's will to evangelize? No, definitely not. This only means we must continually add knowledge to our faith (2 Peter 1:5) and grow "in the grace and knowledge of our Lord and Savior Jesus Christ" (2 Peter 3:18).

We should be like Andrew in John 1:41. As soon as he realized who Jesus was, he first found his own brother Simon, and said to him, "We have found the Messiah." If you had access to unlimited wealth—for yourself and for all with whom you wished share the secret—how many people would you tell about this great discovery? Well, we should feel the same about this treasure of salvation. Who do you want to reach with this "treasure," this "pearl of great price"? We must have the same attitude that the twelve-year-old Jesus had when He said, "I must be about my Father's business" (Luke 2:49).

Tools to Make the Job Easier

Just as there are textbooks and reference books for learning a subject in the secular world, there are a variety of helps available for studying the Bible. Are they absolutely necessary for someone to be able to teach? No. However, they do make the job easier.

Bible

To begin you will need a Bible. There are a number of translations available from which you can select. In fact, there are so many it could become mind-boggling trying to decide. Thankfully, there are some guidelines you may use in helping with this task.

Make sure the Bible you select is a true translation, not a paraphrased or transliterated version. The scriptures were written in Hebrew, Greek, and Aramaic. For most of us to be able to read them, they must be translated into English. A Bible that was translated from the original language manuscripts is a true translation. A paraphrase or transliteration occurs when the writers use another English Bible and put it in other words. You can find this information on a page near the front of the book that you have in question. What's wrong with a Bible that is a paraphrase or transliteration? Well, I'll try to explain.

No language stays the same throughout history. Words become obsolete and many change meaning. To illustrate the point, in the King James translation, 1 Samuel 17:22

reads, "And David left his carriage in the care of the keeper of the carriage and ran into the army." In this verse, what other word would you use to describe carriage? Cart, buggy, chariot, or wagon? When the King James Bible was translated into English (A.D. 1611), the word *carriage* had two meanings. The original Hebrew word used here is *kelîy* (kel-eé): "something prepared . . . implement, bag, pot, sack, vessel." So, you see, a paraphrase (English to English) does not give the true meaning of the verse. The New King James translation reads: "And David left his supplies in the hand of the supply keeper, ran to the army, and came and greeted his brothers." The New American Standard translation reads: "Then David left his baggage in the care of the baggage keeper, and ran to the battle line and entered in order to greet his brothers." Make certain, therefore, the scholars have used the oldest manuscripts available (in the original language of the biblical writers) in their translating and updating of the scriptures.

I know people who think it is actually sinful to use any translation other than the King James Version. They don't use a dictionary, cookbook, gardening manual, medical book, or other literature that was written in the seventeenth century. Why restrict our learning to a book translated during that period of history? King James, who provided the funds for the translation, was not a prophet of God. The scribes he selected to do the work were certainly not inspired men. They were all men who simply felt the need for the Holy Scriptures to be translated into a language that was understood by the people of England—namely, Elizabethan English.

Another fact that many do not realize is that a large number of the passages in the 1611 translation were taken from the Catholic Vulgate manuscripts (a Latin Bible), not the original Hebrew, Greek, and Aramaic of the scriptures. In addition, a lot of Bible readers may not realize that there have been many, many revisions to this translation since it was printed. The King James Bible we read today is not the same translation our ancestors read in 1611.

Make certain the translation was not done by only one person or a group of people from only one denomination. When one person or a group from the same denomination translates, the result may be a translation that has been manipulated to teach a particular doctrine or belief. Choose a translation, instead, that has been compiled by a staff of translators from a variety of religious backgrounds. This helps to assure that the English words are translated as close to the original language as possible. When trying to select which translation is right for you, read a few passages in each before making up your mind. Choose sections of the Bible that you find most difficult to understand, and see if a more modern translation of the words will help you.

Concordance

A concordance is a book that helps locate a particular passage in the scriptures. You do this by looking up a particular word that is found in the verse you want to find. For example, if I wanted to know where the verse is that teaches baptism I would find the following:

> Baptized: Acts 1:5 John truly b' with water; 1:5 ye shall be b' with the Holy Ghost; 2:41 gladly received his word were b'; 8:42 were b' both men and women

This is only a partial list, but you get the idea. The same format is used for all the words in the Bible. One hint that is helpful when searching for a passage is to choose the words in the verse that are not as common as some others in the same verse. To illustrate the point, if you wanted to find out where the Lord said "Go teach all nations," you would use the word *nations* instead of *go.* Why? The word *go* is used 201 times in the New Testament, a lot of verses to search through, while the word *teach* is used only 30 times. Obviously, it would be easier to scan 30 verses than to wade through 201 to find the passage for which you are searching.

There are several companies that make concordances. The most popular ones are Crudens, Youngs, and Strongs. While Crudens is only a concordance, Youngs and Strongs are concordance-dictionary combinations. I'll elaborate on the dictionary function in the section below.

Is a concordance necessary for my salvation? Absolutely not, but locating passages is a lot easier with one than without one.

Dictionary

When we want to look up a definition of an English word, we grab a dictionary (Webster, Collegian, New World etc.). However, as we mentioned earlier, the scriptures were not written in English, but Hebrew, Greek, and Aramaic. If we want to look up the definition of a biblical word, we must use a Hebrew, Greek/Aramaic dictionary. There are many good publications on the market, and only you can decide which is best for your library.

Some books labeled "dictionary" add features found in an encyclopedia as well as a dictionary. *Smith's Bible Dictionary* and *Holman's Bible Dictionary* are two examples.

For example, if you were to look up the word *baptism* in the Holman dictionary you would get the definition and a whole lot more. The definition reads:

> The immersion or dipping of a believer in water symbolizing the complete renewal and change in the believer's life and testifying to the death, burial, and resurrection of Jesus Christ as the way of salvation.

However, the explanation goes on to expound on the history of baptism in Judean history, John's baptism, Christ's baptism, and the baptism of Christians during the New Testament age.

One fact about Hebrew and Greek is that the same English word might have several definitions in the original language. Some dictionaries simply list the different definitions, while others list the meaning of the word in each passage. Strongs and Youngs are two examples of the latter type.

For example, if you were to look up the word *love* in Strongs concordance and dictionary, the table below shows a partial list of what would be displayed.

Love:

Ps. 4:18 I will *l'* Thee, O Lord, my strength	7355
Ps. 91:14 Because He has set his *l'* upon me	2836
Isa. 63:9 in his *l'* and in his pity he redeemed	160
Matt. 6:5 for they *l'* to pray standing in the	5368
Mk. 12:30 thou shalt *l'* the Lord thy God with	25
Jno. 5:42 that ye have not the *l'* of God in you	26
Tit. 2:4a to be sober, to *l'* their husbands	5362
Tit. 2:4b to be sober...to *l'* their children	5388

English Word	Num.	Hebrew Word	Definition
love	160	a-hab-aw	affection
love	2836	khaw-shak	to cling; delight in
love	7355	raw-kham	have compassion; be merciful

Using a book with this format will help you understand what a particular word means in a specific passage of scripture.

Holman's Bible Dictionary gives a definition only on key words and topics. It combines the features of a dictionary and encyclopedia but does a better job in the encyclopedia department than it does as a dictionary. For example, if you were to look up the word *love* you would find: Love:

"Unselfish, loyal, and benevolent concern for the well-being of another." However, several paragraphs examining the topic of love, as found in the scriptures, would follow.

Smith's Bible Dictionary also does a better job as an encyclopedia. In fact, the cover to the book states that it covers "peoples, places, manners, customs, events, doctrines, key words . . . (etc.)." It also comes in an illustrated version, which adds interest to the research by using drawings to illustrate many of the topics discussed.

Is a dictionary absolutely necessary for our salvation? Certainly not, but it does make studying the language of the Bible a bit more easy for the average person.

Topical Bible

A book of this type has passages listed under specific topics. This is particularly helpful if you want to locate all of the scriptures on a certain subject or find every passage concerning a person in the Bible. For example, if you wanted to do a study on pride, a partial list of what we would find, depending on the topical Bible you use, would be:

Pride

Exodus 18:10–11 And Jethro said . . . "Now I know that the Lord is greater than all gods: for in the thing wherein they dealt proudly he was above them."

Lev. 26:19 "I will break the pride of your power; and I will make you heaven as iron, and your earth as brass."

You can also research a particular character in the scriptures. For example:

Ruth: The daughter-in-law of Naomi, Ruth 1:4. Her devotion to Naomi, Ruth 1:16–17 with verses 6–18. Goes to Bethlehem, Ruth 1:19, 22. Gleaned in the field of Boaz, Ruth 2:3. Receives kindness from Boaz, Ruth 2:4–17; 3:15. Under Naomi's instructions claims from Boaz the duty

of a kinsman, Ruth 3:1-9. Marries Boaz, Ruth 4:9–13.
Becomes an ancestor of Jesus, Ruth 4:13, 21–22; Matt.
1:5.

Is a topical Bible necessary for our salvation? Certainly
not, but it is a real time-saver when doing a topical or character study.

Commentaries

Commentaries are available on the entire Bible and on
partial books or characters. Some are written by a group of
men and others by individuals. They give men's opinions
on different scriptures and references. There are many titles
available in bookstores around the country. Here are a few
listed: *Barnes Notes, Bible Commentary* by Zerr, *Gospel
Advocate Comentaries*, *Pulpit Commentary*, and *Halley's
Bible Handbook*.

There are differing opinions regarding their value in
Bible study, but each person must decide whether or not
such a thing is helpful. It might do well to look at them in
this light. We attend worship and listen to the preacher
and the Bible class teacher as they explain the scriptures
to us. A commentary is simply a sermon of sorts in printed
form, to help us with understanding God's will. The responsibility falls to us in checking behind what the writer has
said, by doing what the Bereans did during Paul's time:
"They searched the scriptures . . . to see if these things are
so" (Acts 17:11).

Commentaries can be a great asset to our study. Be
careful, however. Writers, like preachers, are imperfect. They
are not inspired apostles of the Lord.

Bible Encyclopedias and Almanacs

A Bible encyclopedia or almanac is just like any other
encyclopedia, except it deals with topics of a religious nature.
It takes a word, character, or place and goes into more detail
than can be found in the scriptures.

For instance, we find the word *Hittite* in the scriptures. If we want to know more about these people who played a prominent part in the history of Israel, we would be limited by what's revealed in the Bible. However, the word of God was not the only literature being written during that time in history. If we want to search further we must turn to secular writings.

Historians, the Recorders of Events

Herodotus was a historian who lived during the time of the Old Testament. He wrote particularly during the period of the Babylonian and Median and Persian rule of the world. His descriptions of King Darius; King Cyrus; and King Xerxes, the husband of Esther, adds weight to the truth of the scriptures.

Flavius Josephus was a historian who lived during the time of the Roman occupation of Palestine. He observed the plight of the Jews and, at a later date, the persecution of the Christians. He wrote many books which chronicle these events, and four have survived through the ages: *The Jewish Wars* (composed about A.D. 73), *The Antiquities of the Jews* (about A.D. 93), *Life* (an autobiographical appendix to *The Antiquities*), and *Against Apion,* (penned shortly after *The Antiquities*) (*Holman Bible Dictionary,* 1955).

Ever since men have been able to write, they have recorded the life and times of human beings. Other ancient writers also left writings on events that occurred during their lifetimes. Inspired? No, but these manuscripts enhance our understanding of life, as it happened so long ago.

Archaeology, Remains of Former Civilizations

Throughout history there have been people who were fascinated with civilizations of the past. All over the world things like cities, temples, and tombs have been exposed to the public eye. Many ancient books have also been discovered and translated into modern languages. Drawings, paintings, and other decorative art have given us insight into life during the time of the Bible.

Many of these individuals set about to disprove the scriptures but ran into a surprise. Instead of proving God's revelation to be a hoax, they added proof that the Bible is an accurate chronicle of the history of mankind. Not one excavation has provided information that would in any way cast doubt on Holy Writ.

One thing that bothers many students, especially the young students, is the dating of items that are discovered. They are concerned that the scriptures place the age of the world much younger than the archaeologists.

My explanation is simply this: When God created Adam and Eve, they were full-grown and able immediately to have children. We know this by the Lord's command for them to "be fruitful and replenish the earth." The trees He put in the garden were mature and bearing fruit, as soon as they appeared. We know this because God said He provided them as food for the animals and man. How old did Adam and Eve appear to be at creation? What was the apparent age of the mature trees when God created them? Of course, we don't know exactly. However, we do know they were not seedlings. Conclusion? If God created a full-grown man and full-grown trees, why do we seem surprised that He created a forty-billion-year-old rock? Let the scientists carbon-date items all they like. All this does is show the power of our Master in heaven.

Is it necessary for us to study archaeology to understand God's will? Absolutely not, but it can help in making locations, people, and events come alive as we study.

Atlases

An atlas is a book of maps. Some publications are limited to just page after page of maps, while others expound on the regions shown and the people who inhabited the area during any given period in history.

Why would I want to own a book like that? When we read about Abraham's being from Ur of the Chaldeans it is interesting to be able to locate Ur on a map. When we read about the Ethiopian eunuch's being on the "road that runs down to Gaza," we can actually find that road in our atlas. Some people find this helpful to their study, while others couldn't care less where Phrygia is located.

Is an atlas necessary for our understanding of the scriptures? Absolutely not, but it does enable us to "visit" the locations where biblical events took place.

Study Questions

1. What is the difference in a translation of the Bible and a paraphrase of the scriptures? _____

_____

2. What is the function of a concordance?_____

_____

3. Why do you need a dictionary for Bible words that is different from the dictionary you use for general purposes? _____

_____

_____

4. When and why would a topical Bible be helpful in studying the Bible? _____

_____

5. What benefit would a Bible encyclopedia be to your study? _____

_____

6. What is a contemporary historian and how might their works be helpful in studying the scriptures? _____

_____

_____

7. Who was a historian contemporary with the Median and Persian rule of the world? _____

8. Who is one of the more notable Jewish historians of the first century, and what four of his books are preserved for our study today? _____

_____

_____

_____

_____

9. What is an atlas, and how might it help us in examining the scriptures?_____

_____

10. Why would any student of the Bible bother to use the types of books we've looked at in this lesson? _____

_____

Lesson 12

RULES FOR
EFFECTIVE PERSONAL EVANGELISM

What Do I Say First?

A good place to begin is by discussing something of interest to the other person. If they have children, this is a great subject with which to break the ice. If you both have something in common, such as sports, reading, or TV, now would be a good time to have a short discussion about it. Avoid asking personal questions beyond ordinary things, like their place of employment or the children's names.

If there are small children who might prove to be a distraction to their parents, take along someone who can entertain them while you are studying. If the TV is on—many people leave it on so much they don't even realize it—you might ask with a very polite smile, "Would you mind if we turn the TV off? I tend to get distracted easily, and I don't want to misunderstand anything you have to say."

After a brief chat, introduce whatever type of study you've chosen for the session. Be prepared! Always bring your personal Bible, and if you have extras, bring a couple more, preferably the same translation as yours. Always take at least one King James translation, because some people feel it is the only inspired translation of the scriptures. Also bring a pad and some pencils so you can write down any questions or other information that might be necessary. If you are using a slide projector or other audio-visual equipment, check it before the time of the class. If a bulb is burned out, or if there is some other technical problem, you don't want to find it out while everyone is prepared to listen to the material you've chosen to study. Always take extra extension cords because electrical plugs may not be in convenient places.

The Art of Listening

We can become so zealous in our teaching efforts that we fail to let someone else interject their thoughts. Stop talking long enough to give the other person time to talk.

Concentrate on what the other person is saying. If you are so busy disagreeing with him while he's talking, you may not grasp what he's trying to communicate to you, and it is very important to really understand that. Use proper facial expressions while he is talking. Smile but don't overdo it. Look thoughtful, nod your head, and show other signs of listening. In other words, let him know you are truly interested in what he is saying, and that it is important to you.

Don't answer too quickly. The other person may not be through talking. Some people have long lapses between their thoughts and their words, especially older folks. If you speak too soon, you may be interrupting an important thought.

The other person should get the feeling from your attitude that her belief and comments are the most important thing to you at that very moment.

What Should I Say, and How Should I Say It?

The attitude we project can directly influence the success or failure of our efforts to reach lost souls. Things like arrogance, close-mindedness, impatience, or disinterest will get in the way of the effectiveness of the study. People see through pretense and will not have respect for a Christian who seems to be interested in getting the upper hand or winning an argument.

What if the person you are trying to reach uses profanity —it's such a habit with some they do it unconsciously—or does something else you find distasteful? Remember, wrong things result from the influence of sin, and Christ can make any knowledgeable, sincere person as pure and as white as snow. Don't be too verbally critical at this time.

- *Leave your prejudices at home.* If what is uppermost in your mind is what you find wrong with this person— religion, background, skin color, or job—you will not be an effective teacher. Jesus died for all men and women "while we were yet sinners" (Romans 5:8).

- *Start on a positive note and you will accomplish much more.* Do not begin the study with criticism of your prospect's beliefs. If possible, find some common ground on which you both agree. There is truth in all religions, but not all the truth. You might begin on the wonderful act of Jesus' coming to earth so we can all have an opportunity to live with Him eternally in heaven. You might begin with a remark about the blessing of being able to study the Bible with friends without having to worry about being arrested, as were the Christians in the New Testament.

- *Don't feel that errors have to be corrected immediately.* Many of these things will disappear as the person grows "in the grace and knowledge of the Lord Jesus Christ" (2 Peter 3:18). If you try to explain immediately the wrong of all the incorrect statements, you will overpower your prospect with don'ts and discouragements before the gospel even has to chance to produce fruit.

- *Do not react with anger to anything the prospect says.* Some non-Christians will make snide remarks about the church of Christ, about some Christians, or even about you. Some might use this technique to test you and your sincerity. Never, never, never argue about a point of disagreement. One of the marks of a mature Christian is the ability to discuss a controversial subject without becoming argumentative. Paul told Timothy "not to strive about words to no profit, to the ruin of the hearers" (2 Timothy 2:14). Remaining cool-headed will show your prospect that you are truly interested in spiritual things and that your desire is to help others go to heaven.

- *Keep a cheerful attitude.* Don't use this time to tell your prospect about your bad day, poor health, money problems—you get the idea. If your prospect begins to tell you about personal woes, listen with a sympathetic ear. Remind your prospect that God does not take away all our problems in this life, but He has provided help for us to bear them (Romans 8:28).

- *Don't be tempted to use too many passages of scripture.* Your uncontrolled familiarity with the Bible can be overpowering, especially to one who is not familiar with it. One or two scriptures on a topic are usually sufficient to illustrate a point; deeper study will be more appropriate at a later date.

Do Your Homework

Try to anticipate what you might encounter when you engage in a Bible study, and prepare yourself for the task. The first step is to discover where your prospect is on the road to salvation. If you are teaching an atheist, you will have to begin by proving there is a God. If you are teaching a Buddhist or Muslim, perhaps you will begin as Paul did in Acts 17, by teaching them about the true God "who made heaven and earth." If the person is a member of a denomination, you should try to find out something about what they believe: to be forewarned is to be forearmed. Be careful, however, not to say anything to your contact like: "I know you don't believe in baptism . . . grace . . . etc." No one likes to be told what he believes. Use accumulated information only to prepare yourself better for an effective study.

Don't Be Discouraged

We must understand that everyone we tell about the gospel will not listen. Of those who listen, not everyone will obey. Of those who obey, not everyone will remain faithful. Jesus was the Master Teacher, and many turned a deaf ear to His lessons. In fact, He angered some so much that they crucified Him. Are we to say that we want to be more successful than our Lord?

We should remember the words of the apostle Paul: "Be not weary while doing good, for in due season we shall reap if we do not lose heart" (Galatians 6:9). We are on the earth to plant and water, but remember, God gives the increase (1 Corinthians 3:7). The harvest is His. We are laborers in His vineyard. The problem is not with the crop. The problem is with the workers. Jesus said,

> Do you not say, "There are still four months and then comes the harvest"? Behold, I say to you, lift up your eyes and look at the fields, for they are already white for harvest! (John 4:35).

Study Questions

1. What are some suggestions of things you can do to break the ice when you begin a study with someone?

   _____

2. What are some things that might be distractions to a good study, and how would you handle them?

   _____

   _____

3. What does it mean to be prepared? _____

   _____

4. Make a list of the things you should carry when you study the Bible with a friend. _____

   _____

   _____

5. Why should a teacher strive to be a good listener?

   _____

6. When we go to study with someone, what should we leave at home? _____

   _____

Lesson 13

PRACTICE MAKES PERFECT

When we started to learn to walk, ride a tricycle, ride a bicycle, skate, or accomplish any other skill we now take for granted, we were not able to do it properly the first time we tried. If you've ever learned to play a musical instrument, you must have heard your teacher say, "Practice makes perfect."

Well, evangelism is no different from any other skill we want to learn. The more we do it, the more comfortable with it and the better at it we become. Today we are going to practice evangelism through a series of exercises with each other.

In this lesson we will put to use the skills we have studied. We'll do this by performing some role-playing scenarios. This lesson can take place in a ladies' class or with just a few Christian friends in someone's home. There will be no questions at the end of this lesson, but there will be places for you to add some notes as you go along.

Preparation for Practice

Get a small table—a card table will do—and place it in the front of the room. Place four chairs around the table. Furnish the table with a concordance, dictionary, Bible, pencil, paper, a few tracts about the church, and a box of Kleenex. If you're wondering about the Kleenex, they become handy when someone recognizes her condition and feel remorse for her sins. Or there will be some other emotional moment. It happens more than you might think. Now we are ready to begin.

First of all, do not feel embarrassed, silly, or intimidated. We are all women—friends trying to make it to heaven. Believe it or not, these exercises will really help you approach others with the gospel. So all of you be a good sport and participate. If you cannot because you are just too shy, don't feel bad; others will lead the way. After each scenario have an open discussion with the class and discuss how things went. Encourage each person to offer advice as to how the session might have been improved.

Exercise 1

Select two "volunteers" for your first study. One will assume the role of a Christian and the other will be a friend who is a good person but doesn't feel the need to make a commitment to the Lord.

Objective of Christian: To convince her prospect to attend worship services.

Hints for the Christian: Use the concordance to find passages that have to do with what God requires in our worship to Him.

Objective of friend: To convince the Christian that if someone is a good person the Lord really doesn't mean that she has to go to church to be saved.

Hints for the friend: Be creative. Use excuses you've heard others make in defense of your position.

Notes for Exercise 1

_____

_____

_____

_____

_____

_____

_____

_____

Exercise 2

Like our first study, we will assume one is a member of the church and another is her denominational friend. In this instance the friend should ask the church member to tell her about the church the Lord established, and why she attends there instead of someplace else.

Objective for the Christian: To convince the other person that Christ established only one church, and that it does matter what you believe and obey. All roads cannot be right.

Hints for the Christian: Use the study material on the table. Find passages that have to do with the way to heaven. You might start with, "There is a way that seems right to a man, but the end is the way of death."

Objective for the friend: To convince the Christian that one way is as good as another way and that God has left it up to us as to how to worship Him.

Hints for the friend: Use passages that dwell on the mercy and the goodness of God, as well as those that talk about Christian liberty.

Notes for Exercise 2

_____

_____

_____

_____

_____

_____

_____

_____

Exercise 3

In this instance, we will assume that both women are members of the church, but one has fallen away and doesn't attend any longer. She has two small children and has to hold down a job to be able to afford the things in life she enjoys. Her husband is not a Christian, so there is no support there, and her parents live in another state.

Objective for the Christian: To convince the backslider that she needs to return to the Lord and His church.

Hints for the Christian: Dwell on passages that have to do with our not being able to handle life's problems without God's help. Talk about the future of the souls of her children without biblical teaching in their lives.

Objective for the friend: To make convincing arguments that she really doesn't need to come back to church.

Hints for the friend: Use the excuse that many of the problems are really God's fault or church people's fault, and so the church would just be one more headache.

Notes for Exercise 3

_____

_____

_____

_____

_____

_____

_____

_____

Exercise 4

In this scenario one woman is a member of the church and the other is a stranger she finds herself sitting beside in the doctor's office. We have no idea whether she goes to church or has any interest in spiritual matters.

Objective for the Christian: To interest her in a Bible study; to interest her in a Bible correspondence course; to interest her in coming to worship services.

Hints for the Christian: Remember the ice breaker section in a previous lesson. Get her interested in you first; then approach her with spiritual matters.

Objective for the stranger: To be wary of this other person, and to be suspicious of what she's saying.

Hints for the stranger: Be creative. This scenario can take any direction you would like it to take.

Notes for Exercise 4

_____

_____

_____

_____

_____

_____

_____

_____

Exercise 5

This time one is a member of the church, another, a neighbor's child; and the third, the child's mother. The mother is not in the room when you begin talking, but enters later. The child begins to tell his mother what you want to do.

Objective for the Christian: To get the child to attend Bible study and worship. Also, when the mother shows up, to encourage her to come and check out things for herself.

Hints for the Christian: Speak on the child's level and use vocabulary that corresponds with the age group. Do not stress the fun he will have, but emphasize learning about Jesus and heaven. You might also mention meeting other boys and girls who are learning about God.

Objective for the child: To find out why you would want to go to the lady's church.

Hints for the child: Ask questions about what kind of games they have or if you'll get any kind of treats there.

Objective for the mother: To be questioning about someone wanting to take her child to "their church."

Hints for the mother: Be suspicious of this church. Mention things like, "Well, I've heard . . ."

Notes for Exercise 5

_____

_____

_____

_____

_____

_____

_____

_____

Conclusion

Well now, that wasn't so bad, was it? You can continue this kind of practice with your family or friends in your own home. Get your kids involved. You can never begin too early to learn the importance of telling people about the Lord.

Look at it like this. If you knew where anyone could make a phone call or could go someplace to receive a thousand dollars free for the asking, how many people would you tell. How many phone calls would you make? To how many strangers would you pass this information? The kingdom of God has been called a treasure (Matthew 13:44), and a pearl of great price (Matthew 13:46), and it is there free for anyone who will come. Isn't the knowledge of how to obtain this great prize important enough to share with everyone who will listen?

True, they will not all listen, and they will not all come. But we are like the watchmen on the wall in the cities of old. God told them:

> If you warn the wicked, and he does not turn from his wickedness, nor from his wicked way, he shall die in his iniquity; but you have delivered your soul (Ezekiel 3:19).

Again He said,

> Because you did not give him warning, he shall die in his sin, and his righteousness which he has done shall not be remembered; but his blood I will require at your hand (Ezekiel 3:20).

While we are not living under the Old Testament law today, God's attitude has remained constant down through the ages. We do not have an option. We must each try to reach others with the gospel, and as we try we can remember, "Practice makes perfect!"

Now grab your needle of determination and begin weaving in your life this thread of love that runs throughout the Bible. You and God are a majority. As you work with Him, He can make wonderful things happen.